M000104865

The Man Plan

A Guy's Guide To Planning The Perfect Date

by Mariann O'Connor & Sharon Sommerhalter

The Man Plan, a Guy's Guide to Planning the Perfect Date © 2013 Mariann O'Connor and Sharon Sommerhalter. All rights reserved.

No part of this publication may be reproduced, digitally stored, or transmitted in any form or by any means, electronic, mechanical, photocopying, recording or otherwise, without the prior written permission of the copyright holders.

First Edition
First Printing, 2013

LifeBytes™ Publications

Cover and interior design by Sharon Podsada

ISBN 978-0-9892715-0-9

Dedications

Sharon:

For the angel on my shoulder, Lorraine Marie Sommerhalter. Thank you Mom!

Mariann:

My mother's words inspire me every day, "Mariann, there's nothing you can't do if you put your mind to it." Thank you for always being my biggest supporter!

Table of Contents

Section 3: Other Useful Information

ACKNOWLEDGEMENTS

We would like to thank the many friends and family who support us and are always happy for us. Thank you to our beta-readers who took the time to provide thoughtful and honest input. They really helped us focus and we appreciate it. They include Nikki Petty, Robert Golder, Michelle Di Felice, Mark McGreevy, Mary Angela Flood, Peggy Gillespie, June Tireman and Richard Valois. Special thanks to Joann Lamneck for her support.

James Dolan – thank you so much for being our editor on The Man Plan™ and meeting an aggressive schedule. You're the best.

Rob Golder has never failed us with his support from being the king of clever titles, to providing many laughs at Mariann's expense to being "headshot central." Thanks for your friendship and loyalty.

Thanks to Donna Frosco for always having our back! You always keep a watchful eye over us and for that we are eternally grateful!

We would also like to thank Jonathan Bird at SinglesWarehouse.co.uk for his continued support and unbelievable generosity in promoting us and our writing projects!

Sharon:
I would particularly like to thank my family for not rolling their eyes too blatantly when I get involved in another one of my creative endeavors. I send special thanks to my dad Otto Sommerhalter and my son Ryan Podsada for always being my biggest fans on this publishing journey. You are my anchors and my rocks, and I love you all.

Mariann:
I want thank my Mother and Father (Patricia & Ken O'Connor) for showing me love, giving me faith and confidence, and being a great example in perseverance. I love you both and know you are watching over me from heaven. To my family and friends who always smile with enthusiasm and cheer me on at the smallest success in my creative pursuits – Thank You!

FOREWORD

As the founder of the on-line dating sites, SinglesWarehouse.co.uk, DatingSmarter.co.uk, and several others, with members throughout Europe and North America, I have been promoting and discussing on-line dating and relationship issues for a long time. Over a year ago, I got to know Mariann and Sharon, authors of "The Man Plan™ – A Guy's Guide To Planning The Perfect Date". They were fast gaining recognition for the quality and substance of their writing and advice on their LifeBytes™, Real Stories blog when I asked them to write a weekly article for Singles Warehouse magazine as one of our Singles Warehouse Experts. It has been a great partnership ever since and I'm happy to say this book is an informative and entertaining next step for Sharon and Mariann in their growth as writers and dating experts.

I deal with tens of thousands of single people and many single men seem to be in a quandary as to how to plan a date and what to do for the woman they want to get to know better. This book, The Man Plan™ – A Guy's Guide To Planning The Perfect Date, provides all the tips, elements and ideas to get you started on the road to planning the perfect date. This book is for men, but when I read the book I thought one of the first things I am going to do is give a copy to my girlfriend and ask her to pick her top 5 favorite dates from the book and then I will surprise her. So, it is written as solid advice for men but it can be used by women as well.

Dating can be a minefield in the 21st century and you'd be a fool not to take good advice. From date planning to actual dating tips "The Man Plan" will guide you down the right path. Witty and to the point, this book is the ultimate survival guide to the dating world.

Jonathan Bird
Singles Warehouse

— Section 1—

10 TIPS

FOR DATE PLANNING

How To Plan The Date

Planning a date can be a scary thought and may give you night sweats just thinking about what to do or where to go with that special girl who you are trying to connect with — or get into bed. Do not fear. We know dating is not easy and planning a date can be a nightmare. But, it's a necessary evil. You have to do it, so you might as well become expert at date planning. Before long, friends will be rushing to you for advice. Don't worry; we are here to help you. You are not alone in this endeavor. We (Sharon and Mariann) have years of experience dating, planning dates and sitting through too many horrible dates. We write blogs and articles on dating and relationships. Most importantly, we are women and know *what women want*. So, trust us. We are going to get you through this. Just take a deep breath and keep reading.

There are worse things than having to plan a date. Believe us! A woman loves a man who can take charge and plan a date, and with our help, you will become an expert. The first thing to remember is, there is a fine line between taking charge and being controlling. Taking charge is *good*. Being controlling is *bad*.

Some women love to plan dates, and that is wonderful. Let them. But, for a first date especially, we think it's best if you take the lead. Women will be impressed by a man who can take charge, be original, and illustrate his planning skills. Women find that sexy — We know we do. And it could help seal the deal. The ultimate goal is to make the girl you are meeting, like or are trying to connect with feel special. Regardless of what women say, they want to feel like a Queen, that they are special and that you love them or at least like them enough to put some effort into creating a special night for them. It feeds into the romanticism that women have about finding Prince Charming. It's an aphrodisiac.

Women can be forgiving. The date does not have to be perfect. You get huge points *just for trying*! Everything could go wrong but your lady will appreciate the effort and find it cute and amusing if things go awry. One of

Sharon's former loves took her on a romantic weekend in the country to a hotel that boasted hot tubs in the room. Her boyfriend made sure to have flowers and champagne in the room before they checked in. He sweetly left a card on her pillow. Unfortunately, the room, which had seen better days than what was represented on the internet, had the hot tub plopped smack up against the bed. Her boyfriend was horrified. But, Sharon laughed her butt off and thought it was just charming. Not perfect, but almost even more romantic. Like we say, *women are forgiving.*

You will face plenty of opportunities to execute your date planning skills. But first, we are going to share 10 tips for Date Planning. These elements should be considered for any date regardless of how casual or formal it is or where you are in your relationship.

1 Determine Your Dating Goal

You are going on a date. So what? For some serial daters, it is just another night out on the town. For hopeful romantics, it could be the first night of the rest of their lives. A date is a big deal. This is your first chance to make an in-person first impression. Dates take an investment of time, money, planning and caring. Maximize your results by giving it the respect and attention it deserves.

Ultimately, you have to determine what is the end goal of your date. For example, is it to just get out and not be alone? Get laid? Propose? Realize statistics are on your side and you could be meeting your soul mate? Spice up your current relationship? Tell your friends who are pressuring you to meet someone that, yes, *you are dating and going out*! Or is it to make your lady feel truly special?

Be honest. You don't have to make excuses. We have all been in various places in our life and wanted different things at different times. People go on dates for all kinds of reasons. Sometimes it's because we're looking for love and sometimes we're just looking for company. Know the purpose and end result you want from the date and that will help you set up the date you want.

If this is a casual first date to see if you have chemistry, very little planning is required. If this is a special night date, then you really have to understand what kind of experience you want this to be for you and your love. In this case, a lot of thought and planning goes into the execution of the date. If this is a spontaneous fun date, you may not have a lot of time and need to act quickly. If the ultimate goal of this date is the bedroom, then you'll want to make sure the entire date feels like sexy foreplay.

Once you know what your budget is, the kind of date you want and the goal of the date, you can start to put a framework around building and planning your date.

2 Know Your Budget

Whether you are watching your budget or have money to spend, it is always a factor in planning any date or event. It is not always the amount you spend, it is the originality and thoughtfulness you bring to your date.

We recommend going more *economic* or *middle of the road* on the first date. This is your first meeting, and you are not sure there is going to be a second date. First dates are nerve-wracking, so the simpler the better. Your main goal is to get to know her and not to break the bank. As you get to know the person and want to make outings more special or memorable and you have the cash, by all means spend what you want.

Dates are expensive. Even an average cocktail can be pricey. Wine can be $10 a glass and an appetizer $8-$12. If parking or tolls are involved, you can easily spend $50-$60 a date. If you go on two to three dates a week, you can spend $400 to $500 a month. The totals add up very quickly. If that's like pennies to you, then you are very lucky. But most people have bills and many have kids or alimony to pay, so their discretionary funds for social outings are limited. Don't feel bad if you have expenses and need to keep finances in check. Also, many women feel uncomfortable if first dates are too expensive or too formal. There is an "expectation" they feel that puts added pressure on the first date. You don't want your date to feel this way! But, don't let this inhibit you from taking that gal out on a special first date for a really nice dinner at a great restaurant. She will appreciate it. Just don't make comments indicating you have *expectations* as that will make her feel uncomfortable.

Be prepared — there are some women who expect a 5-star first class date from the get-go. Why? Well, because that's what they expect from a man. Agree? If you do, she may be perfect for you. Just make sure you don't resent that expectation from her because it won't stop there. You may find her challenging, and if that revs your engines and intrigues you, then don't let her go. Personally, my time is valuable and I don't want to sit through a three-hour 5-star dinner making small talk with someone who may not be for me. There is time for fancy dinners after the first date when I decide if I want see the guy again. I can meet for a drink or go for coffee or appetizers and determine if I want to go out on another date. But, if someone wants to treat me to the top French restaurant or Sushi Bar in New York City, then sure, I'll go. At least I will know he's not cheap, which is a pet peeve of mine!

I know one man who brought flowers to his first date, which is a great idea. But, then for each subsequent date, he brought his girl some kind of gift. Yes, that is very generous. But, that "generosity" can set a precedent early on and establish unrealistic expectations for the guy and makes it weird for the girl. Flowers on a first date are a romantic and a sweet gesture. A gift on each date looks like you are trying to buy the persons affection, and that is just awkward and could send the wrong signals. You don't want to do that!

As the relationship progresses, there are times when you may want to make a big splash. Figure out what you want to do and the associated costs. Consider if you can achieve the plans for the evening cheaper, if you are watching your budget. Do not go into debt to plan an elaborate date. I have done this and it is a very bad idea especially if the relationship does not work. You will be alone with only your high credit card debt. That is not only lonely, but depressing as well.

Most women understand that men have financial obligations. But, if you consistently exhibit cheapness on your dates, that could ruin a relationship *if* it's a girl's deal breaker. For one on-line encounter, Mariann went out for dinner on a first date to a TGIF (Thank God It's Friday) restaurant with a cute guy. She drove in from New Jersey to meet him in New York City for dinner. They sat at the table for an hour, and her date kept motioning for the waiter to come back later. Then, he suggested they split an appetizer. Mariann was somewhat disappointed since he invited her to dinner and she was starving. She was enjoying his company as they sat at the table for another two hours talking and agreed to a second date. On a $21 check, he left $3 which was barely 15% and tied up a waiter's table for 3 hours. Having friends in the food service industry, this is a big "no-no." It made Mariann question his level of consciousness and thoughtfulness since he invited her for dinner and she got half an appetizer and then he left less than the lowest tip you should leave. These were red flags that made her cautious when they went out on their second date. Mariann felt so bad for the waiter, she returned to the restaurant and gave the waiter $10 and thanked him for being so pleasant and not rushing them. Her on-line match and she dated for about a month but the chemistry, unfortunately, just wasn't there.

You can do a lot for free or very little money. Just check out the **Budget Dates** in the book. But, to give you an example of what things cost, here is a summary so you can get a snapshot of how much you will spend for different types of dates.

Coffee	$6	Drinks at a Bar	$28
Dessert and Coffee	$12	Appetizers & Drinks	$50
Casual Dinner for two	$80	Walk around a Fair	$15
Movie with Snack	$30	5-star Dinner	$250 - $300
Nice Dinner	$150	Broadway Show	$150 - $250
Comedy Club	$75	Opera / Ballet	$100 - $250
Picnic	$10 - $25	Bowling	$30 - $60
Ice Skating	$0 - $20	Apple Picking	$5 - $30
Political Lecture	$0 - $10	Cabaret	$100 - $200
Jazz Club	$50 - $125	Sporting Event	$30 - $150
Hotel	$100 - $300	Wine Tasting *(per winery)*	$12 - $20

3 Find The Perfect Venue (regional magazines, papers, on-line)

You are about to move beyond the *thinking* stage to the *doing* stage. Once you know your budget and the goal of your date, you can start to determine the location and timing or any other elements you want to involve.

It is recommended that you know your local restaurants, wine bars, music venues and lounges. Not sure? Well, start with a regional magazine covering local happenings or places to socialize. One can often pick them up in local stores or hotel lobbies. Practically, everyone has a computer and a smart phone, so it is easy enough to get on Google or Yahoo and find restaurants or activities that would help fill in the framework of your date.

If you are going to meet for coffee on a first date and want it low key, then find a cozy Starbucks or Barnes & Noble. Start to investigate where some cultural venues are whether it is a museum, jazz club or free Shakespeare in the Park. Adore the outdoors? Find some pretty hiking trails or somewhere to go kayaking or to play tennis — perhaps you could find *Love:Love* on the tennis court! Point. Set. Match!

Be an investigator. Don't think of it is as a job. Think of it as an exploration into fun and knowledge. It is like a treasure hunt where every search on the internet or turn of a page can lead you to an idea or experience that could be memorable, special or just plain fun. Stay alert and keep your eyes open for advertisements or cozy places that could serve as the backdrop to a romantic evening. Let your mind and imagination open wide, and be receptive to not only your surroundings, but to things friends say, things your girlfriend loves to do and even your own likes and dislikes or activities you would like to try.

This is the major portion of the battle. Most people claim they don't have good ideas or are not sure where to go or what to do. It's easy, just listen and look around you. As reference for future dates, set up a few folders and compile notes on the outdoors, vacations, seasonal events, cultural events, organizations, music, food and anything that interests you or think will interest the person you are doing all of this for. Pretty soon, the ideas will flow, and you will look forward to planning new and interesting dates.

4 How Romantic Do You Want To Be?

There is a fine line between a romantic gesture and going so over the top you make your date uncomfortable. Again, where you are in the relationship will dictate your level of romance.

If it is a first date, we suggest something subtle and not obvious. We know one red rose is considered cliché, but it is actually quite sweet and romantic. If you have both shared a joke or something meaningful in your emails or phone conversations, then taking action around that would be appropriate. For example, Mariann loves "Rudolph The Red Nosed Reindeer". She always cried when Yukon Cornelius went into the abyss with the Bumble. Of course, after many years as a kid watching this, finally her mother said, *"you do realize finally they don't die, right?"* And, yes, Bumbles bounce, so Yukon Cornelius lived and so did the Bumble, which was great because he was tall enough to put the star on the tree back at the North Pole. It was Christmas time and Mariann was corresponding with someone on-line who was a big movie buff. She had a few email exchanges about favorite movie lines and she said her 2 favorite movie lines were, *"Bumbles bounce,"* and *"Lookey what he can do"* (spoken by Yukon Cornelius when the Bumble put the star on the tree at the end of the movie). They met in New York City for their first date and he brought a snow globe of the Bumble placing the star on the tree. She thought that was so funny and thoughtful and made her want to give him a chance because he seemed to have a good heart. The relationship didn't last, but the gesture was kind and romantic.

In another on-line exchange, Mariann met someone who called himself *Three-A-Mangos*. They emailed a few jokes about mangos and she laughed when he gave her three mangos on their first date. She admits she stopped laughing and thinking he was sweet when he told her after dinner that he had a girlfriend and hoped they could have a threesome. Yeah, Mariann wishes she was joking on that one too but, unfortunately not! She walked out and told him to keep his mangos. If in doubt, refer to **Chapter 6 (Organize Your Talking Points)** on appropriate date conversation.

A small bouquet of flowers always works, as many women are a sucker for flowers. You have to decide if you want to have a romantic gesture on the first date. If you don't, that's fine. It is not necessary or may make you uncomfortable. You can always amp up the romance if you continue to date. If you feel a connection and want to make a gesture, all you have to do is acknowledge something that has meaning to her or both of you. And, if you can't come up with anything then go with the flower!

On your first date, don't go overboard with gifts. This is a date, not Christmas. So serenading that lady with a singer and violin and jewelry at dessert might be too much. Roll it back a bit - OK, a lot! If you are dating for any time, any romantic gesture is always appreciated and could land her in your arms or your bed! If you do too much, then it takes away from the *special feeling* a sweet and simple gesture can bring. Your romantic gestures should have a surprise or sincere element and not be expected.

5 What To Wear?

What you wear can speak volumes about you. Do not under-estimate the importance of your clothing. Dress for the occasion. If you are just going for coffee, that tux might be a tad too much. The key to what to wear is to dress appropriately for where you are going. Most women love to dress up. They tend to like to play it cool, casual and low key on a first date where they can wear nice jeans and a sexy top and look thrown together in a very deliberate sexy casual way.

If you are meeting for drinks right from work, just make sure you are both business casual. If you work for a utility company and are high atop poles negotiating electricity, then go home and get into a pair of Dockers and a button down. If you are going hiking, then wear something that is appropriate for hiking. If you plan on doing something after hiking and won't be going home to change, let your date know to bring something to change into. Women love men who are clean and nicely dressed whether it be a suit, casual or funky cool. Trust us, just make sure you don't have sweat marks on your shirt.

Recently, Sharon went out with someone who wore a shirt that was so wrinkled and dirty, she lost her appetite. Then, when he raised his arm, the repeated yellow stains from under arm sweat were calling to her like a shining light. She wanted to flee and never see him again. His clothes spoke volumes about his lack of cleanliness and personal care. Sharon surmised that if he didn't take any care with himself, he most likely would not with her either.

Don't get us wrong, women don't mind men who don't have the ability to coordinate. They may try and fail, but the woman will give them 100% credit for trying and might actually think it's cute. If she wants to take you shopping to help you buy clothes then accept and go and have fun with it. She will feel like she is helping you and before long, you will look even sexier to her.

Now some guys can pull off the torn jeans with the cool flowery shirt, very manly belt and hip shoes, but many can't. The worst thing you could do is think you are one of those guys and not be. Therefore, if in doubt, ask a few friends. If you are not yet a fashion forward icon, then enlist the help of a friend with some cool fashion sense to make improvements on your clothing choices. If you are not sure what to wear, go clean, simple and put together – the woman will give you the benefit of the doubt. If you have the money, then hire a stylist for a makeover. At the very least, remember that simple things mean a lot. Wearing sneakers to a first date says *ultra casual*, while wearing nice leather shoes says *classy*.

Are you one of those guys who likes very specific clothing or hair styles on women? If not, then you can skip this paragraph. If you are, then please keep your opinions to yourself until you get to know the girl and if she's accepting of your input. Mariann had a date who told her she looked like she dressed for a job interview. That didn't go over well with her as she was coming from work. Another date told her he didn't like her scarf and would have gone with higher heeled shoes. Mariann doesn't mind hearing this from girlfriends but not a guy who she doesn't know well. When she hears comments like that, it usually masks a man who should be dating ... *men*! Get to know your date and if she is receptive to your input, then great. But, do not be or appear controlling or inflexible. One guy Mariann dated told her that her hair-style was all wrong and started to finger it like he was a hairstylist. It freaked her out and she lost any attraction she had to him. Some men have a very good fashion sense, but how that is conveyed to the woman he's dating and when and how often can be critical in having a happy relationship.

When you see your lady, it is always nice to acknowledge that she looks nice. If something stands out like shoes or a necklace or dress, then be vocal and let her know. Women love compliments. Do not be insincere because women can sniff out insincerity quicker than a dog on a hunt for food. Also, don't go so overboard that you make her feel uncomfortable as that can appear too needy or anxious. That can be extremely unappealing to many women.

If you have been dating for some time and want to take your lady out for a night out on the town, then by all means tell her to dress to the nines or wear a sexy cocktail dress. If you are surprising her for the evening, then one sexy maneuver is to have a dress sent over to her as a gift from a nice boutique or department store. If she chooses to exchange it, then be fine with it. But, the look of the dress will indicate the kind of evening you have planned. And sending it as a gift will make it an even sexier night. Just don't ruin that by including lingerie with the dress. Let the night happen organically and don't set up an expectation or obligation.

6 Organize Your Talking Points

What to say on a date to someone you do not know can be the most nerve wracking experience known to man. Where do you start? What do you talk about? What topics should you stay away from? How much is *too much information*? These are all good questions that you should have the answer to before sitting across from your date. What you say in person on a date depends on how much you have talked before or how much information you exchanged on-line or how long you have been dating this person.

If you are calling the person for the first time, we would suggest keeping it light and having an internal time limit. Keep a little mystery and get off the phone with them craving more. Talk about family, jobs and travel. Do *not* talk about ex's or your therapy sessions or the last time you had sex. These are all topics you should wait to discuss. End the conversation by asking for a date. Definitely propose a day and time and try to get it confirmed before you get off the phone. If she says she has to check her schedule, then give her a couple of days and follow up if you have to without looking too anxious. If you promise to call, please do. There is nothing worse than a guy not calling when he says he will. It hurts, and you don't want to hurt someone's feelings!

If you are meeting in person for the first time, try to be complimentary without seeming fake. Be a gentleman — you'll get big points for this. Be on time and have a positive attitude. Don't come in complaining about the douche bag that cut you off in the parking lot. Be cool, calm and confident. And remember to *smile*. Women are a sucker for a light-hearted guy with a nice smile and great sense of humor.

Before you go on your date, try to have some talking points or topics you might want to talk about so you are not left with a *deer in the headlights* look. You may decide to talk about family, vacations, work, travel, favorite pastimes or funny experiences. I would not talk about your bitch ex-wife who slept with your best friend. Or, lament over your parents' divorce. Or cry over how you only see your kids every other weekend. Buck up, be a man and make this a fun experience. It is *not* a therapy session. Your date is not your therapist. Sharon had a friend who went out with someone she'd met at a party and half way through their first date he cried, literally cried, to her about breaking up with his last girlfriend. Needless to say, that relationship did not work out.

How do you change the subject? Gracefully and casually. If your date is talking about her ex or complaining about him, you respond, *"aren't you lucky you are free from him and that negativity. What kinds of things make you happy or what do you do for fun?"* Or, if they start bashing the President of the United States, then just say, *"Politics is politics. Whether I agree with a politician or not, I try to respect the office, be it the President, Senator or state official. Funny I visited Washington DC recently and revisited all of the memorials and forgot how beautiful they were. Do you like architecture or art deco style? Do you have a favorite city?"* And if your date is overstepping bounds and asking a question that is too personal like how many women you have been with, you can respond, *"A gentleman never talks about his ex's. But, I am enjoying being here with you. What is the most important quality you want in a friend? Boyfriend?"* Changing the subject is all about deflecting what was said with an objective comment and turning it positive and asking a question forcing them to answer the question. Honestly, if after three times they won't get off a topic, you can nicely say, *"I would rather discuss this topic when we know each other better, if you don't mind."* How they respond can tell a lot and after this date you may decide to move on to the next person.

Have a script in your head but be flexible enough to go with the conversation and respond to what is being said. If you see the conversation veering into an area where it can get awkward or uncomfortable, then be sensitive to the signs and steer the conversation in a different direction. They always say *do not talk about religion or politics*. That is true, but Mariann has broken her own rule on that. Sometimes, she has been pleasantly surprised that they were on the same page and other times terribly disappointed that they were not. If you do make some comments and you have different viewpoints, then do not enter into a volatile exchange nor should you yell, insult or lose your temper. Just agree to disagree and move on. If you get closer, then perhaps you can discuss those topics with a more level headed and respectful approach. Just remember that you need to extend the same respect and courtesy to your date as you want extended to you. Mariann once went out with a guy that looked like Bobby Kennedy who was cute and very nice but oddly enough, all he did was talk about politics. Now, they agreed on several (but not all) issues. After a while, she wanted to expand the scope of their discussion to include family, values, hopes and dreams, work, philosophies of life and be able to laugh and be silly with him. But just talking about an inactive Congress did not do that for her.

If you are talking to your date and you feel connected, then great. Keep it going. But, if you feel no chemistry or connection, then the best thing to do is keep the evening short and always remain respectful and gentlemanly and part ways in a gracious manner.

There are two secrets we are going to reveal to you that will make you sexy, desired and loved by women. Are you ready? They are:

LISTENING

ASKING QUESTIONS

If you *listen* to your date, she will notice, and that scores major points with her. By listening, we don't just mean with your ears. We mean with your body, your eyes and your attention span. Do not look up at every person walking by. Don't be easily distracted with your eyes darting around the room. Lean into your date and show her you are there 100% to get to know her. Look directly into her eyes and notice the color or if they smile when she does or if they dart away (she could be nervous) or what kind of soul lies underneath. Does she stare right back at you? If she does, then you may be sharing a very strong connection.

Mariann and Sharon's biggest pet peeve is men who do not listen or ask questions. When you meet someone, make it about them and be sure you show interest in what they are saying and let it be OK if they do all the talking. Conversation is not a one sided endeavor. It is meant to be interactive and a two-way street so you both get to know about each other. If you don't ask questions, then you don't learn about your date and you wind up talking completely about yourself. You don't want to appear self-absorbed or egotistical. When you ask questions it illustrates you are present and listening. Curiosity also shows your date you are interested in them and want to know more. If you do, then you will find the exchanges more lively and enlightening. When you are talking, just be conscious *not* to interrupt or talk over your date. You may be anxious to say something, but let her finish her sentence or thought and then speak. Mariann admits to being guilty of this and has had people do it to her and she hates it. So, she tries hard not to repeat that bad behavior. It takes effort, but all good things do.

Mariann recently met someone on-line. They started to chat on the phone and she asked the first few questions about his experience with the site and on-line dating. He did not ask her the same question. Then there was silence. That was awkward so she asked a question about his family. He answered and again did not ask her anything. There was more silence. So, she asked about his job and travel schedule. At that point, he said, *"Let me tell you a little bit about Jim"* (name changed to protect the ridiculous). For the next 48 minutes (yes, she was looking at the clock), he talked nonstop about himself, his hobbies, his travels and his job. Mariann stupidly asked, *"Where have you traveled to for your job?"* He then spent 10 minutes listing every city he had been to in the United States. It was during this boring list that she went to the bathroom, made tea and fixed a snack and when she returned, he was up to the W's on the list of work destinations. At one point he told her he went to Hawaii and had been to all the islands except

Kauai. She anxiously chimed in before being cut-off and noted, *"I was just in Kauai and it was beautiful."* He said nothing. There was about 20 seconds of silence and he then said, *"Well, anyway, my favorite island is the Big Island … blah blah blah …"* He did not even acknowledge what she said nor did he ask what she liked about Kauai, where she stayed or if she liked the food. And if that wasn't bad enough, over the course of 48 minutes he told her that he loves to shop for lingerie. OK, so Mariann's inner sarcastic voice wanted to ask if the lingerie was for him but she refrained. He told her this three times. In case you were wondering — that is too much information and very inappropriate for a first conversation. Mariann got off the phone as fast as she could. Unfortunately for him, he did not exit the conversation without making himself look really pathetic. She mentioned that she had dated someone from the site and it bothered her that he never offered to take her garbage to the disposal in her condo community. This is where he told her that he was like a cocker spaniel and would do anything he was asked and he liked to be told what to do so he did not have to think and he was easy to train — like a dog. In case you were wondering, this is not attractive nor is it sexy. Women want to date a man, not a dog.

If you listen, you will learn about your date, and in doing so it will help with future date ideas. When you listen, you hear the subtext, the tone and what is spoken between the lines. You see the heart of the person and if she is kind and thoughtful or selfish and abrasive. Listening is not only sexy to your date, but it helps you figure out if you want to spend more time with this person. When you ask questions, you show you are interested and engaged, and that is very attractive to a woman. Again, it is important to find out about the person without appearing like you are a police investigator. The exchanges allow you to determine your compatibility and give you a hint as to how you communicate with each other and what you have in common.

We recommend you don't share too much information, especially initially. Get to know the person without being intrusive. It is OK to share hopes and dreams and show your silly and intellectual side. Keep the conversation moving and if there are sticking points or awkward subjects, move on quickly to another topic. Once you break the ice and get to know each other, then conversations will flow more naturally on future dates. As you get closer, you can share more information and opinions.

If you listen and ask questions you will have a successful date! And more importantly, you will have a thriving relationship and marriage. When you ask questions, don't make it sound or feel like an interview. Remember, it's a conversation. Here are some topics you may want to find out about your date initially and over the course of a few weeks:

Job	Passions	Siblings
Hobbies	Sports Interest	Like the Outdoors
Favorite Music	Favorite Colors	Enjoy Funny Comedies
Travel	Favorite Destination	Vacations
Background	Close to Family	Best Friend?
College	Enjoy Culture	Prefer Casual or Elegant
Children/Visitation	Marital Status	Goals and Aspirations
Life Philosophy	Funny Stories	Favorite Comedian
Favorite movie	Favorite Play	Favorite City
Love at First Sight?	Pet Peeves	Change about Herself?
Smoke	Drink	Relationship Deal Breakers
Spending Money	Dog vs. Cat	Frugal or Spender
Her best Quality	Her best feature	What Feature Attracts Her
Volunteer	Got a Bucket List?	

Here are some things you will need to eventually find out if this relationship is expected to continue:

Heart-broken	Religion/Religious	Political affiliation
Drugs	Physical condition	Mental Health
Criminal Record	Debts	Sexual History/disease
Intimacy Expectations	Handling Finances	Value System

Here are some topics that are *not appropriate to discuss* on a first date:

Sex Life	Exes	Sexual positions
Number of partners	Money in bank	Offer threesome
Her anatomy	Your therapy sessions	Your anger issues

As you get to know the woman you are dating, the boundaries of your communication will change accordingly and you can talk more in depth about a plethora of topics.

7 Plan Your Date Strategy

If you want victory on your date or in your relationships, you need a strategy and a plan to achieve the highest level of success and satisfaction. Think we are exaggerating? *"Come on, don't be ridiculous. That is stupid. This is not a business."* Yes, we can hear your thoughts. Really, we can! You are a business. Whether you are at a job or in school or trying to find your one true love, you are a business. You have a goal and need an action plan to accomplish that goal.

For example, if you have met a woman who intrigues you enough to pursue her then you really need to think about the person and how you are strategically going to win her heart. Is she the kind of girl who hates games and just wants to be pursued? Does that lady you like thrive on being mysterious and make winning her heart a challenge? Do you want to start out slow or go full force and come on strong? In order to determine the best approach, you really have to understand the girl you are chasing. We personally hate games and both like to be pursued. Mariann and Sharon both agree they don't like guys to come on too strong. Mariann prefers a slower pace that allows her to be fully in touch with how she feels. If someone comes on too strong and her feelings are not commensurate with theirs, then she feels uncomfortable and backs away from the relationship. If they had just paced it slower, then the relationship might have worked. Of course, this is like a double edge sword. Mariann once dated a guy she really liked who took it slow and she became increasingly attracted to him. But, he continued at such a snail's pace that she felt the relationship stall and the sparks wane. If he had a strategy, the relationship might have been successful. It was fine going out once every other week for a month, and then three times a month, but after six months, she wanted to see him more than once a week for just dinner. He took it so slow, that it became stagnant and Mariann felt unimportant in his life. Next to work and his kids, she was not a priority. He did not go out of his way to make more time for her and that spoke volumes to Mariann about this man. Turns out emotionally, he was not what she needed and felt he was stingy with his feelings in that area as well.

Sharon prefers a guy who will step up and more quickly show his interest and be honest with how he feels. If she has been dating someone long enough to consider it more than a casual relationship, she expects her man to be an active partner, be communicative and be willing to work at making the relationship the best it can be. If she does not feel it happening, she will be quicker than Mariann to bring it up to her date.

You need to ask yourself a list of questions, and those answers will dictate your strategy. But, that strategy is definitely up to you. You need to determine if you want to:

• Continue dating casually and low key
• Step it up and plan more dates
• Insert more romance
• Go on dates to spend more time with her
• Go away for a night
• Get very romantic
• Introduce to friends and get third party opinions
• Play it cool – Don't be needy and mess it up
• Show her she's more than special
• Surprise her with something big and meaningful
• Say I Love You
• Propose
• Call it off
• Light a bigger fire and go bold

Take it slow — but not too slow. Don't get overwhelmed. Listen to your heart and your head and you will be fine. Don't dismiss your friend's opinions but don't let what they say over-ride how you feel or what you know is right for you.

8 Be Original

Original is good. Don't be afraid to be original. Remember the one single rose brought on a first date? The thoughtfulness trumps any cliché element – so go for it! We feel many times people get lazy in life with their jobs and in relationships. Once you get lazy, complacency starts, then boredom steps in and then trouble follows. It's OK to be original and to think outside the box. And yes, to even think inside the box on occasion. Make your date different by putting a new spin on an old idea. This will help keep your relationship fresh. Go ahead and plan a date that is silly or elegant or somewhere in between.

Sharon once gave a gift to someone but made up a modified game of Deal Or No Deal and it was cheesy and fun and silly, but it worked. And they laughed a lot! For her nephew's high school graduation, Mariann gave him $500 in dollar bills and coins. She went to the dollar store and found many college freshman appropriate items she could hide money in. She then wrapped each one and put them into a big box. It took a good twenty minutes to open everything, but her nephew always remembers it and laughs because he loved the silly lightheartedness of the gift's presentation. One time, Sharon made up a series of clues and conducted a shortened scavenger hunt. In planning an excursion, for two weeks prior to their get together, she sent daily notes in the mail with clues as to where we were going, which was a surprise. So think of planning date activities differently. For example, instead of going to the movies, plan a picnic with cheese, crackers, mini sandwiches, wine and an iPad downloaded with her favorite movie and watch it under a shady maple tree. Yep, you could have gone to the movies, but this was a more interesting variation on an old idea.

Our litmus test is, *will this create a memory?* Mariann and Sharon love to create memories that last. Therefore, take any simple idea and think about how you can customize it for your girlfriend and make it special. Granted, this does not have to be done on every date. By being original and thinking outside the mundane confines of life, you will keep your relationship invigorated, exciting, fresh and fun.

For something simpler, write a poem and print it out on a nice piece of stationery (you can buy nice stationary at any office supply store like Staples or Office Depot) and then put the poem in a simple frame. You can get a cute frame at a dollar store or discount store for $3-$7. Then, mail it to her office or home or give it to her on a date. Not a writer? OK, that's fine. Then ask yourself, *Does she have a favorite song lyric or specific verse that you could print and frame* or, *does she have a favorite poem or writer that you can copy a poem or quote from?* or, *does she love old books?* Go to the used section of a book store and find one she would like and just leave it with a post it note for her — simple and inexpensive, but original.

If you want to go big and you have the budget, time or creativity, then you can plan a date that is more intricate like renting out a small movie theater and playing her favorite movie. Or, re-enact a scene from her favorite movie. The lesson here is that you think about an idea, and then ask yourself, *How can I make it different or customize it and make it personal for her?* Let your mind sit with that question and an idea may come zooming into your brain or it may take a few days. Don't rush yourself to have an idea. If you relax and think about, the ideas will flow!

9 Learn How To Romance Your Date

Men, please listen. Women love romance. Trust us on this. We don't care what they say. Yes, they may resist and get all "Gloria Steinem" on you, but they love romance. We suggest that whether you are dating or married, you realize and understand the importance of keeping it fresh with your lady. You must learn how to court your date. Yes, that means putting her on a pedestal, oozing charm and being suave, sweet, thoughtful and considerate. I know, I know, it's a tall order. But it is a fun skill to learn and you will reap the benefits every time. By benefits, we mean *Benefits!*

Again, courting does not always mean grand gestures and huge expenses. Romance and wooing a woman is letting her know you care, are thinking about her and are finding a way to express your love. This is really important. Keep in mind, just listening to a woman is an aphrodisiac. Like we said, it can be pretty cheap to win your lady's heart. Is your lady frustrated at work and she can't even get out to a movie? Then do something that eliminates a stress from her life. For example, do her grocery shopping, have a meal prepared for her one night, pick up her dry cleaning, or even do some light cleaning in her home. Or, get a gift certificate to a movie theater to see a movie when she *does* have the time.

One of our biggest problems with dating is that after a couple of months, life becomes routine. And once in a routine, it is much harder to get out of it. We recommend not letting yourself take that road to *boring* and *dull*. Guys tend to put in little thought or effort when getting together. Quickly, your life becomes about staying home and watching a rerun. It is very important to experience life not only as a single person but also as a couple. Many of our couple or married friends will hear about our many outings or adventures and the first thing they say is, "we never go out anymore or do anything interesting." This is very, very bad. Because then your lady will think the grass is greener on the other side, and the other side will not include you. If you are down with this, then by all means, be a couch potato who is not open to experiencing life. But, if this is not you, then get up and use your imagination and ensure that you do not lose this person or yourself.

When you experience life, you start to look at the world very differently. You realize how precious life is and that you can't let it pass you by. Experiencing life does not have to be a drain on your wallet. Go to a free concert, a fair, a political lecture, an adult education cooking class, a museum or an eclectic music venue. Mariann took some members of her family on a *Do Something* weekend. She gave the gift of being around each other in a fun and pretty environment with a few spa treatments, dinner and drinks thrown in for good measure. Create that memory. Keep yourself alive and your mind and body active. Once it goes dormant so too can your relationship.

Also keep in mind, by the mere fact that women are women, they will reciprocate. This will not be a one-way street. Your lady will return the thoughtfulness — OK, so it may take a few weeks after the shock of you being *just the best boyfriend or husband ever* wears off and then you will find that keeping romance alive will sustain you as a couple. Trust us, being "courted" by a man is a true aphrodisiac to us gals! It will strengthen your respect and sensitivity to each other. When that exists, love abounds and your whole attitude is more positive and ultimately, you have a happier life. See how simple that is? If you just listen to us you will be destined for nothing but a happy life!

The key here is to keep yourself connected to that person you are dating. Go and enjoy life, be active and stimulate each other physically, intellectually and sexually. Feeling naughty? No problem! Go for drinks and then visit an adult toy shop like the Pink Pussycat in New York City and buy a few playfully fun toys to test out and see if they were worth the purchase. It does not take a lot to romance your mate and keep your relationship flourishing. It should not be viewed as a chore but a fun challenge that you will *both* enjoy!!

10 Relax. Have Fun. Be Yourself.
(PS: Don't give up!)

Need we say more? This is not only the most obvious piece of advice that anyone can give but it is the best advice anyone can give. At the end of the day, you have to be who you are. You can only fake it for so long before you are found out and the relationship crumbles. Look, we are all on our best behavior in the first months of a relationship. That is not what we are talking about. If you are fake or try to be something you are not or someone you think others want you to be, then ultimately the real you will show its face and heart. Now that may solidify the relationship or your lady could go running and screaming into the night. But, it's a chance you have to take.

Mariann loves a great debate, doesn't mind a good argument and is honest with her friends. But, when she is dating a guy, forget it, she hates confrontation and discussing difficult topics. She assumes anything that bothers her won't change and she walks away. She doesn't even give the relationship a chance to succeed or him a chance to speak up or change. That is unfair. Her friends tell her that when she first starts dating, they don't know where the real Mariann goes as she tempers her humor and personality. This is disingenuous and that is bad. After the first stage of dating passes and the veneer of trying to be perfect wears off and you can't be who you really aren't anymore, the real you will show up to dinner and bed and events. So, either the girl you are dating will like you or not. If she does, then wonderful – just enjoy getting to know one another. If not, move on as there are more women than men out there so your chances of finding "Ms. Right" are very good.

If you are a complete narcissistic jerk, then I suggest you stop dating and see a psychiatrist. Really! It's not all about you so get yourself in order and then enter into the real world once you know how to be a decent and humble human being where you can exhibit love and respect. Who knows, once you do, you may live happily ever after!

The one last important thing to remember that we will emphasize is – Do Not Give Up. If you go out on dates and love is not happening for you that is OK. Just hang in there. You have to trust us on this. You might have to change your venues, strategy or go for a different type of girl, but there is someone out there for you. Check out **What To Do Between Dates in Section 3** of this book for ideas.

Mariann and Sharon are veterans of on-line dating and meeting people at parties and activities that interest us. Recently, Sharon convinced one of her best friends to try on-line dating. He did. He is at the *over analyzing every profile* stage. Yes, this happens initially. Once your skills are honed, you can go through the profiles pretty quickly to determine if someone interests you. After four weeks on-line and five coffee dates, he is in a state of despair and disillusion. She tries to tell him this is the tip of the iceberg — to have hope and keep the faith. It is hard, but if you give up you have nothing. When you try, at least you have the *potential* of something good happening. So, don't give up. Make sure you don't just rely solely on on-line dating. Participate in life and get yourself off the computer chair and out into the real world meeting people. Chalk it up to experience and the journey you had to take to meet your one and only. In time, you will.

Mariann laments that she has been on numerous dates and questions if she will meet her soul mate since she is still single. And, yet her brother met four people through the personal ads (yes, before on-line!) and he is married 20 years to the girl with Box # 4291 – only his fourth 4th date through the personals. Good for him. She is happy for him and his wife as they are a perfect couple. Mariann loves them and their wonderful children and thanks God every day for them in her life. Yes, she could question that why after many years she can't meet someone and yet her brother met someone after four first dates. She realizes, that is life. Everyone has a story.

Maybe hers was to write this book and share her years of knowledge and experience with people. Maybe her guy is number 218. Mariann doesn't know, but she perseveres and does not give up.

When a date does not work for us, we keep moving forward. When it does, we both have gratitude. That is all you can do. Have fun and gratitude and stay in the game. In time, life will give you all your dreams.

Cost and Romance - Symbol Guide

We have tried to put an associated cost and romance level with each date group. It is approximate and many times it is subjective. As for the cost, it can vary depending on where you live. In a rural town, socializing will cost less. In big cities, it is more expensive to date.

Again, you don't need to spend a ton of money for off the charts romance. The date ideas in the book are varied so that you can go all out or cut back and exercise a budget version.

Budget Guide:		Romance Guide:	
$	$0 - $50	♥	Fun and Nice
$$	$50 - $100	♥ ♥	Lively with hint or romance
$$$	$101 - $500	♥ ♥ ♥	Romantic with potential for more
$$$$	$501 - $1000	♥ ♥ ♥ ♥	Sexy and Very Romantic
$$$$$	$1000+	♥ ♥ ♥ ♥ ♥	Off the Charts Romantic

— Section 2—

DATE IDEAS
TO GET YOU STARTED

Date Ideas For Every Occasion

This section outlines different types of dates with suggestions for each date group. It is not meant to be a complete listing of date ideas, but is a good place for you to start. Hopefully, it will get your creative juices flowing and then you can expand on these ideas and build dates that are fun and original around activities suitable to you and your lovely lady! You can plan a date exactly as outlined in the book, mix and match from the various dates, or tweak a date incorporating your idea that makes it perfect for your girl. This is a great first effort in planning the perfect date. If you nurture romance and making your girl special and a priority in your life, she will do the same. Dating is a 2-way street and if she does not step up or takes you for granted, then you may want to consider one these dates on someone who deserves it.

1 The First Date (\$ /♥)

The first date. She said yes – congratulations! Don't sweat it. Keep it simple. You can't be faulted for simple on a first date. The 30th date in your relationship perhaps, but not the first. Take a breath and keep your primary objective in your sight — *to get to know your date.* You are on a mission to determine if you have met the love of your life, someone who should be a friend, a living nightmare or a funny story at a cocktail party.

DATE	COST	ROMANCE
The Coffee Date	\$	♥
A Walk In The Park	\$	♥
A Drink By Any Other Name Is … Just A Drink	\$	♥

Things to consider:

• This is the 1st date to get to know your new lady. Low key and inexpensive is OK.

• Arrive on time and spend 1-2 hours max. Have an open mind.

• Arrive early and get a table if you are meeting at a coffee shop.

- Buy the coffee for your date. If it's a *walk in park* date, bring coffee or water with you.
- Check out local area wine bars or music venues for a drink.
- Don't go too big. If you want a romantic gesture, bring one rose.

Things you may need:

Bring your personality, an ability to make conversation, coffee, rose, and your manners.

All you want to find out on a first date is:
- Does the person look like their photo, if you met them on-line?
- Does the person appear like the one who wrote you emails? Or seem the same outgoing person you met at that party last week?
- Are you attracted to this person?
- Do you want to go out again with this person?

Those are the only four questions you have to ask yourself. At the end of the date, you should be able to answer all of them. If you can't, then you did not do your "due diligence" which is after all — *your job*!

When you are on your first date, keep the conversation light. Find out the essentials:
- Are they single, divorced, widowed or separated? Be subtle and don't delve too deep into these areas.
- Do they have children? If yes, how often do they see them?
- Do they have a big family? Many friends? (Just a word of caution — we don't trust people who are on bad terms with everyone in their family or who have no friends and are loners).
- Do they work? Where? Do they like it? What is their dream job?

You'll want to find out the above information subtly and under the context of an interactive conversation. This is not an interrogation or a job interview. You are not a police officer and she is not a criminal (that role playing comes a little later in your dating cycle!). Don't pull out a pad with questions on it. Yes, I know what you are thinking *who would do something like that*? Well, Mariann had it happen to her — the loser pulled out a list of questions from his briefcase. Yeah, you read right, a briefcase! If you do, then that is a surefire way to stop any future relationship dead in its tracks. Reread **Tip 6: Organize Your Talking Points in Section 1** for information on how to prepare your first date conversation points.

For example, you can ask the following in a conversation without looking obvious:
- If they have a big family?
- For a funny sibling rivalry story?
- Do they travel a lot and do they go on tours?
- Do they have friends they travel with?. If they say, *"I have no friends, I travel alone all the time"* — well this is a red flag you need to be cautious of!

We strongly recommend you not talk about your ex or who you hate or all the problems you are having at work. Keep it light and positive. Share information or any "baggage" in time and when appropriate. Don't do a "data dump" on the first date – it could scare them off. (A "data dump" is when you tell every piece of information about yourself and your life).

Dates are expensive. If you are watching funds, then by all means keep your first date to an affordable and quick meeting. Do not make your first date hours long. Keep it to 1-2 hours and if you are interested — ask her out for another date. Always better to keep her wanting more. Besides, if you are on the move or have things to do it shows you have a life and a schedule. At the same time, if you like her, you can show that you have the manliness (OK, so I wanted to say *balls*) to step up and be proactive and ask her out, which is sexy and romantic.

A. The Coffee Date

Yes, the *Coffee Date* can be considered cliché, but it works and it achieves your objectives. Most importantly, the girl you are meeting will find it perfectly acceptable albeit unexciting. Sharon prefers The Coffee Date as a first meeting with men she's met on internet dating sites. Since it's the first time she and her date actually lay eyes on one another, she's found it to be a fun, low stress way to see if there's anything there for either of them that will warrant a second (or what she calls "a real") date! Mariann hates coffee dates and prefers the opportunity to get dressed up and meet for a drink. Your date *will* expect more planning on future dates and I know you will not disappoint. But, for about $6.00 you can determine if you have found your future wife, a fun lay or crazy in the making. Pick a Starbucks or local coffee place that has chairs and a couch (preferably).

Tips to remember:
- Buck up and pay for the coffee. Do not make the girl pay.
- Get there early and make sure to get a table.
- Keep your conversation light.
- Don't overstay your welcome. Keep them wanting more.
- Do not run away if you find she looks like an alien or twenty years older than her on-line headshot. She will be scarred for life. You are welcome to be honest and tell her that she should post pictures that more accurately represent her. But, always be a gentleman.
- If this is someone you met at a party, function or a fix up through a friend, then give them a warm hug hello and refer back to meeting them and how much you enjoyed their company.

B. A Walk In The Park

Do you have a park near you that is pretty at any time of year? Does she enjoy exercise? Let Mother Nature be your background and grace you with her beauty. Ask your date how she likes her tea or coffee and bring her a cup. Does she have a dog? Tell her to bring it. It will make her feel comfortable and relaxed. Spend an hour and see if her inner and outer beauty matches with what Mother Nature has provided. If yes, end the date with a warm hug and a request for a second date. If a kiss seems natural and appropriate, then go for it! Tell her you will call, and *please* do! There is nothing more disappointing than a guy asking to go out and you agreeing and then he does not call. It hurts. If you don't mean it, then don't ask!

Tips to remember:
- Bring her coffee, tea or something cold if that's her drink preference.
- If she brings her dog, show you are comfortable with animals. Bring a couple of doggie treats. It shows your thoughtfulness!

- If you are *not* interested in her, that is OK. Dating is numbers and statistics. Maybe you should think about expanding your parameters and going for different types of girls than your norm.
- Hopefully your date goes well. If not, perhaps you made a friend or at least got a funny story out of it.

C. A Drink By Any Other Name Is … Just A Drink

Who doesn't love a cocktail? OK, except perhaps for a teetotaler. If your date is a non-drinker, then go to a coffee or juice bar. Otherwise, go for a wine tasting at the local liquor store and pick out a wine for your next date. Is there a cool bar in your area with a band, or a cozy wine bar with a sparkling fireplace? Or an Irish pub that makes you feel like family? As a first date, this should be a short one too but it lends itself to lasting longer if you are really hitting it off.

Tips to remember:
- We will caution you to keep to two drinks especially if you are driving. You don't want the girl seeing you in stripes or an orange jumpsuit by the side of the road as it may not be your best color or pattern. Once you have three drinks, you tend to talk too much or regret too much.
- Pick a place that is not too loud so you can hear each other talk.
- If you are not picking her up, choose a place convenient for her and in a safe part of town.
- Walk her to her car afterwards.
- If you are unsure what to do, give her a hug. If your conversation or evening has gone such that you can give her a kiss, then do.

2 The Second Date ($ to $$ / ♥ to ♥♥)

The second date is tricky and promising. You want to spend more time with her, but still want to watch your budget and don't want to get elaborate in your plans. Do you really like this girl and know it? Or, do you think she might be cool but need some more time with her to determine that? How you feel about the girl can determine what you do. Remember, you're still getting to know one another at this point.

DATE	COST	ROMANCE
Dinner — Ya Gotta Eat	$ - $$	♥
Taste The Grape	$	♥
Music To Your Ears	$ - $$	♥♥

Things to consider:

- This second date is to get to know your lady better. You can step it up a notch and keep it affordable.
- If it's a dinner date, keep it comfortable and casual.
- Ask her what cuisine or restaurant she favors unless you remember from a previous conversation.
- Don't let her pay for the date, even if she insists.
- Check out local bars for a new band or karaoke bar.
- Don't go too romantic. But, ask for that third date if you are interested.

Things you may need:

List of bars with bands, karaoke listing, makings of a picnic basket, winery trail map.

We don't mind a simple date. Sometimes the simple dates turn out to be the most romantic But, even with simple plans, it impresses us when our man spends some time thinking about what to do. If you've been listening, then you have a good idea of what places and activities your newfound love enjoys. Start there in your planning for date number two! Whatever you do, don't leave it up to the woman and make her plan the date. This is your job.

Tips to remember:

- If she volunteers an idea without prompting, by all means go with it, and you can add your own special touches to the date if you want.
- You can certainly ask if she has any ideas or something she would like to do. If she does, she will tell you. If she says, *"No, surprise me"* (that means, come up with an idea and just plan a date and don't ask me for an idea), or *"I'm open to anything"* (she's flexible but don't take her on another coffee date), then just plan the date.
- We would strongly recommend you do not take her to a movie.

A. Dinner — Ya Gotta Eat

Dinner is a solid second date. You don't have to go 5-star – nor would we go in the opposite direction and walk her into a fast food joint or delicatessen. Is there a cuisine she likes? Always try to incorporate what she told you (when you were listening — you were listening right?) into the date. For example, did she mention she loves Indian food? Well, ask her to dinner and say, *"I know you said you love Indian food and I know a great place that I think you will like."* In one sentence, you have told her you were listening (this is huge), are open to doing what she likes, are thoughtful and share interest in the same cuisine. These subtle messages *will* be received. She may verbalize it to you and even if she doesn't, know she will be giving you kudos to her friends.

Tips to remember:

- We suggest picking her up. If you met on an on-line dating site and she is still unsure about you picking her up, just know she is being cautious. She may prefer to meet you at the restaurant.
- If she is meeting you, then try to pick a place that is close to her or at least equidistant between the two of you.
- You asked her out so you pay. If she offers, tell her *Thank You* but you asked her out and it's what a gentleman does. Convey to her you know the right thing to do.
- If she insists, do not give in. Just say — *"Thanks, really. But, I got it."*

Today many women seem confused on when to pay. They want to appear independent or as if they are not taking advantage. Also, they don't want an implied obligation to exist with a dinner. Women need to learn to just say, *"Thanks!"* If the relationship progresses and your new gal asks you out as her treat, then by all means enjoy yourself and hold onto your wallet.

A few more tips:
- Check out her table manners. She will be checking out your table manners too; please make sure yours are good. If someone has disgusting habits, it will be a deal killer. Do you eat with your mouth open? Shovel food in faster than you can chew? If so, stop!
- Remember to pull out the chair for her.
- Ask if she would like an appetizer even if you don't.
- Let her order first.
- Make her feel comfortable in ordering. Don't make comments about how much everything costs.
- Make sure her wine/water/soda glass is full or if there is anything she needs.
- Be sensitive and attentive to her.

Manners really do matter. Mariann went out on a first date with someone who wiped their mouth with their sleeve and openly belched through appetizers without even saying, *"Excuse me."* He belched like it was a badge of honor or that it was impressive. It was not. It was absolutely disgusting and she wound up fleeing the date. You'd be surprised, good manners will go into the PRO column when she is figuring out whether to date or sleep with you!

B. Taste The Grape

Most people love wine. And unless the person does not drink wine, then wine tasting is a great relaxed way to get to know each other and encourages interacting and natural conversation. Visit 1-2 wineries where your total wine tasting intake is no more than two glasses of wine – if you are driving (unless you have a car service or there is a wine tour bus). Make sure to eat, so why not pack a picnic lunch or choose a winery that can prepare a picnic lunch for you or has food available? Bring a blanket and some small sandwiches or cheese, crackers and wine and spread out under a big maple tree or by a lake or a scenic area of the winery and have fun. If you want to limit your wine tasting so you can have one glass of wine with your picnic, then that is a great idea. Who knows, you may both be feeling the chemistry and it might be the perfect setting and timing to go in for that kiss.

Tips to remember:
- Don't get drunk.
- Make sure to get food at the winery or pack a picnic basket (which could be sweetly romantic).
- Have an alternate plan if the winery has a private event and you can't get in.
- Don't get too tipsy and too *hands-on* with her.

If you don't live in an area with wineries, then perhaps you have an apple or fruit picking farm that you can visit and still pack a picnic lunch. We recommend this type of date if you really hit it off on the first date and had chemistry. If things seem to be moving a bit slower, it would make a great third date.

C. Music To Your Ears

Not into the traditional dinner? We understand that. You want something a bit more cool or casual and eclectic? Well, find a cozy bar that has live music, preferably in the genre that she likes, and go for drinks and appetizers. It gives you a chance to chat, relax and enjoy the intermittent music as it offers up moments where you do not *have* to talk. Are you a bit shy? It is a great way to have a break from constant conversation. Have a friend who plays in a band? Yet, another great way to get to know her in a low-pressure environment that is friendly and familiar. Music moves the soul. How great it would be if you both hit it off and made it *your thing* to find new bands or music venues that you like?

Tips to remember:
- Don't get drunk especially if you are driving.
- Don't let her pay. You are taking her out.
- Consider going to a karaoke bar and letting go. Maybe you can performa a duet together?
- Make sure she gets to her car or home safely.

3 The Third Date ($ to $$ / ♥ to ♥♥♥)

To get to the third date means you really like this girl, and she likes you. That's great! But, it's still early and you're both trying to figure each other out and gauge *how much* you like each other. Keep in mind, many girls will use the third date as the date to offer to pay. I would pick something that was not crazy expensive unless you have no intention of letting her pay *if* she does offer. You know each other better now and nervousness should be replaced by excitement. This date is a time to delve more into each other's life, likes and thoughts. Don't make it negative or like a therapy session. Be honest, but be strategic and positive.

DATE	COST	ROMANCE
Movie – There I Said It	$ - $$	♥
Comedy Club – Men Love Women Who Laugh	$ - $$	♥♥
After Dinner Drinks — At Your Place	$ - $$	♥♥♥

Things to consider:

- This date can range from stepping up the romance to sleeping together depending on how fast you are moving. If you do, make her feel special and be sensitive if she is feeling awkward or unsure.
- Women tend to offer to pay on the third date. Therefore, pick an affordable place or pick your choice but don't let her pay.
- If you go to a movie, be sensitive you don't hit a trigger or sensitive point with her (e.g. Cancer / a relative could have just died of cancer).

Things you may need:

List of comedy clubs, dessert, candles, iPod/speaker, wine, coffee, clean sheets, condoms, movie listings.

In New York, the third date is considered the *sleep with* date. We don't follow this rule. Don't assume your girl will either unless your activity on date 1 and 2 make sex on the third date a given. The anticipation of intimacy is something to savor and have fun with. Keeping the mystery and the game of the pursuit alive can be titillating and sexy. Don't rush; enjoy the anticipation of getting your date between the sheets.

A. A Movie — There, I Said It

We love movies but Mariann hates to go to the movies for a date. Unlike Mariann, many people love going to the movies on a date and getting caught up in the drama, humor or suspense. It is a good way to learn about what each of you like or how you respond to the different characters. As long as there aren't a lot of talkers surrounding you in the movie theater, sitting in the darkness holding hands while you stare at a huge screen can be sweet and romantic. Pick a theater with comfortable stadium type seating. Make sure to ask your girl if there is a movie she would like to see specifically. If not, ask what genre she prefers. If she tells you she hates horror movies, don't take to her to Texas Chainsaw Massacres III! Be sensitive to what is going on in her life. Allow enough time to get snacks and get seated.

Tips to remember:
- Arrive early for good seats.
- Offer to buy her snacks even if you don't want any.
- Be sensitive and don't pick a film that has an emotional trigger point for her (i.e. Cancer/accident).
- Switch things up and go IMAX or 3D.
- If you are enjoying her company, ask her for coffee or a drink afterward. Have a place in mind to go to.
- Consider dinner before the movie.

Keep it relaxed, low key and light. If you or your date are classic movie buffs, see if there is a theater near you that's featuring a classic film festival. Sharon loves old movies and old art deco theaters. A date once took her to a beautiful old theater in our area that was showing one of her favorite flicks from the Forties. It was a great date as they could discuss not only the movie, but also the actual theater itself afterwards.

B. Comedy Club — Women Love Men Who Laugh

For Mariann, coming from an Irish family, the philosophy, "laughter is food for the soul" was practiced quite often. She grew up around very witty people who could give as good as they got. So, for her, someone with a sense of humor is critical. If they cannot see the irony and humor in themselves and life, then she doesn't want to get serious with them. No,

Mariann doesn't need a joke machine, but prefers someone who is light hearted and fun. Many women like a man with a sense of humor who can put them at ease.

Tips to remember:
- Make sure to confirm reservations at a comedy club.
- Be on time so you get good seating.
- Check out the comedians to ensure they will be what your date likes.
- There is usually a food or drink minimum at comedy clubs, so take that into consideration when planning anything before or after.

Have a nice dinner before and then enjoy a few drinks while you laugh your butt off. You can end the evening there or keep moving and grab a dessert and cappuccino at a cute coffee bar. Comedy clubs are all around. If you live in a city, there are plenty of comedy clubs or improv groups. If you live in the suburbs, many hotels have comedy clubs or nights on specific weekends throughout the month. Just Google it and you will soon discover where the laughs await you.

C. After Dinner Drinks — At Your Place

Depending on how fast the relationship is moving or whether you subscribe to the *sex on the third date* philosophy, the third date is critical. We always feel the third date is when you decide if you are going to end it or, if the budding relationship has some steam and is ready to move forward. If you are not in the mood for seeing a movie, you may want to go for sushi or a casual dinner and then arrange to have drinks and dessert back at your house. You will need a little preparation for this. You should get a dessert you know she likes and have coffee or wine or a liqueur ready and waiting if she so desires. To create the right ambience, plan to have some candles set up. When you get back to your place you can light the candles and get cozy on the couch.

Tips to remember:
- If she offers to pay, you can let her. So, pick an affordable place.
- Don't push to have sex. It must be consensual. Make sure she is not drunk if she does.

- If you are intimate, then eliminate awkwardness and just make her feel special. Call her afterward.
- If you think it will wind up in the bedroom, have candles and clean sheets. And, if you want to add romance, have rose petals thrown artistically on the bed.

Sometimes relaxing at home and getting cozy on the couch where you can kiss or go further can be a better evening than if you had gone out and spent $3000. If your date gives the signal at all that the third date is too soon to make love, then back off. You can still have a romantic night making out. She will appreciate your sensitivity and when it is meant to happen, it will.

4 Always A Student ($ to $$$ / ♥ to ♥♥♥)

Some people love to do anything that involves learning or getting involved in a new activity. We think this is good because it makes them curious and illustrates their search to keep their mind and body active. If you are lazy, this lady might be the perfect match for you as it will get you off the couch and active in life. Don't be afraid of a woman like this. If you are a person who loves to learn and try different things then good for you, grab your gal and take her along for the ride!

DATE	COST	ROMANCE
Sculpting Class	$ - $$$	♥♥♥
Dance Class	$ - $$	♥♥♥
Cooking Class	$ - $$$	♥♥
Science Center	$ - $$	♥

Things to Consider:

- These dates are for people who consider themselves a couple and really want to explore existing or new interests together.
- It is a bonding experience and you should make it as romantic and flirty as you can.
- Have fun. Your job does not depend on it.
- You can check your local paper or internet for classes in any area of interest for your area.
- Just Google the topic and location (e.g. Science Centers / Maryland) to find venues near you.

Things you will need:

Supplies as dictated by the class (tools, dance shoes, etc.), wine, a great attitude to learn and have fun, confidence, enthusiasm.

A. Sculpture Class

Think of the movie "Ghost" and you can see how sexy this sculpture or pottery class can be. Homework could be sizzling hot! We are sure there is an art school or adult education near you where you can find a class to take sculpting lessons. Check your paper or the internet for lessons or classes. It is a novel idea and at the end of the class you will have something to call your own that represents your artistic spirit. If you and your honey get married, your work of art can take a place of pride on the mantle.

B. Dance Class

Dancing has become increasingly popular thanks to the show "Dancing With The Stars". Dancing can be a great way to not only enjoy, but also get close to your partner. It's a good workout also. You can find a dance school where you can take one or a series of lessons. Whether it is a two-step, line dancing or sexy salsa moves, you can practice your dance steps at home during a romantic evening or go to dance club. Some schools are very specific to the kind of dancing they have. It depends on where you are, but if you Google what you are looking for then you will find something that will suit.

C. Cooking Class

Cooking is useful, yummy and sexy. Whether you are a great cook, a James Beard wannabe or can't even boil water, cooking lessons are a great place to start. From adult education classes to cooking schools to restaurants, you can find venues that will offer a one day lesson or a series of lessons. Depending on how much you want to learn, your time availability, commitment level and available funds, you can choose from taking an Italian Cuisine course that spans four weeks to a one day session in *How to Make Sushi*. Not only is learning cooking skills useful, but it can be a wonderfully bonding couples experience. If you're both "foodies" you can continue to explore cooking techniques – but in your own kitchen. So, get an apron and some knives and rush to the nearest cooking school to learn a new craft!

D. Science Center

Are you dating a geek or someone who just loves science? Well, find a science center near you and visit. You can learn new things about science, biology and technology. Many science centers have interactive exhibits that can be diverse and enlightening. You can learn and laugh – how better to spend an afternoon with someone you have great "chemistry" with?

5 A Night In ($ to $$$$ / ♥♥ to ♥♥♥♥)

Do you feel like you are always going out and are tired of having to be somewhere by a certain time where there are far too many people? That's OK. We all have those nights where staying *in* is far more attractive. You don't have to be out and about to have a delightful evening. You can certainly have plenty of sexy going on by staying inside the four walls of your home.

DATE	COST	ROMANCE
Game Night – Ooh La La!	$ - $$	♥♥♥♥
Deal A Meal	$ - $$	♥♥
Dress Up To Stay In	$ - $$$$	♥♥♥
Fantasy List	$ - $$$	♥♥♥♥

Things to consider:
- These dates can range from relaxing, recharging and G-rated right up to hot, sexy and X-rated.
- These dates don't require too much planning. You may have to buy a few things in advance, but nothing you can't do on-line or go to the store for – so just a couple of hours.
- Play up the romance and sense of fun.

Things you may need:

Sexy Twister, deck of cards, bedroom board games or flash cards, sexy toys, wine/champagne, makings of a meal, recipe book, bubble bath, candles.

A. Game Night — Ooh La La!

Our friends love to have game nights where we play Pictionary, the writing game and other board games. But, believe us, you two love-birds can also play your own games. You can entertain each other with couples games from sexy Twister to strip poker. If you want to do a little planning, find some adult board games that you can play together. If there is a store near you, great – have a shopping trip with your gal. If not, then thankfully you have the internet. So, whether you play Dirty Minds, Indecent Proposals,

The Kama Sutra Game, Dirty Dice or Truth, Dare or Bare, there are plenty of steamy games to keep you entertained and satisfied. Instead of having your friends over for a game of charades, have a party of two for something a little sexier. You can prepare a few appetizers with your favorite cocktails.

Tips to remember:
- This date is not about a meal. It is about exploring a sexy evening together in a fun and silly manner.
- If something is proposed or presented that makes your date uncomfortable, respect her and pass over it. Don't make her do anything she does not want to do.
- A couple of weeks before the date, order some of the games (or go to a store if one is near you) so you have them ready for the date.
- Don't just jump into the games. Set the mood at your place. Sit down, relax, have a cocktail and talk as all this is foreplay. Once it gets a little more romantic, you can bring out the games or make suggestions.

Suggestions and information:
- For the actual games, you can certainly get on websites like Lingerie Diva *www.lingeriediva.com/lingerie-accessories/adult-board-games* or Board Game Central *www.boardgamecentral.com/games/adult.html*.
- Most of the games range from $10-$40.
- Want something a bit edgier, get Fetish Fantasy: Honeymoon Bondage Kit, but I don't think you really need to be on your honeymoon!
- Want to explore your adult fantasies, try The Enchanted Evening, where you spend the evening together exploring adult fantasies and desires as you roll dice and make your way around the game board and each other. This is a sexy game you won't want to miss!
- If you'd like to play a more G-rated game, then try Men are from Mars, Women are from Venus. In this game, it's Venusians (women) vs. Martians (men) as each team tries to guess how other players will respond to multiple-choice questions in seven categories, including "The Dating Circuit," "Communication," and the sex-related "In the Flesh." Women try to match how a male opponent might answer a query from Mars and vice versa.

- Want to go erotic, then there is Advanced Sex Techniques Game, which is a game of erotic foreplay offering over 100,000 possible sexual adventures. Spin the spinner to select tonight's adventure. Begin with sensual foreplay for him and her, then onto erotic foreplay for each of you. When you are both ready to explode with desire, move on to Round Three: Sex Positions.

The variety of games is amazing. You will find something that will spark your interest. Something tells us you will be building up an appetite so make sure to have snacks in the house or see if there is a Chinese restaurant that is open late and *delivers*.

B. Deal A Meal

Stay in and cook and then enjoy the meal together in the comfort of your own home. If you don't know how to cook – no problem! There are lots of easy to follow recipes available on-line, some of which are included in this book under **Sexy Recipes**. Find something easy, elegant and appetizing. The important point is you are doing something together.

Tips to remember:
- Together, figure out what type of foods you are in the mood for.
- Not sure? Look on-line or refer to a recipe book. Don't have a recipe book? Get one in advance from the bookstore.
- Make up a grocery list together, and head to the food store.
- Don't forget the wine. To make it more interesting, get smaller bottles and do a "wine pairing" with your courses.
- Enjoy following the recipe and have fun cooking together. *Do not take control* over the kitchen. If your gal does, just remind her this is more fun as a team effort.
- Pick an area to eat whether it is the dining room, deck or in front of the fireplace – that is up to you two.
- Steal a few kisses in between the logistics of cooking — it will keep the night flirty.

If you have some time to kill while something is cooking in the oven, then perhaps you can get something smoking on the couch! But, I think you will find the collaboration of cooking much more fun than eating out. If you want to add a little sizzle to the evening, spend the evening cooking in your underwear, or just in an apron — yep, that's your call too! If the meal does not turn out well, then just make sure you have a pizza delivery place on speed dial.

C. Dress Up To Stay In

Love to dress up but don't feel like stepping out in the cold? No problem. Get all dressed up and have a sophisticated evening at home. Whether you plan the meal and someone cooks it or you have it catered or you order a tasty pizza delivered all warm and cheesy, it doesn't matter. The juxtaposition should prove entertaining. This evening is about having a *night out* but while you *stay in*. Do some play-acting. Pretend you are in a high-brow restaurant or a honky-tonk bar. Pick a theme that strikes a chord with you and your lady that will be entertaining!

Tips to remember:
- This date is about having fun, relax and be romantic. Its main focus is *not* the bedroom, unless that is what you both want.
- Lounge on the couch in each other's arms watching your favorite movie.
- Or, if you are doing a theme, say the Roaring 20s, then dress up, enjoy the food and then watch some old movies.
- Don't feel like watching a movie? Put on some old tunes and grab your lady's arm and slow dance.
- Have a hot tub? Then end the evening relaxing in each other's arms.
- If you have the budget, hire a service that stages the date for you.

With this date, the fact remains, you don't have to spend a fortune or go outside your home to find a perfect evening at home!

Suggestions and information:
- Need some assistance creating a style and ambience in staging the date? One company in Los Angeles ... *By Michelle* is capitalizing on a need for this. With their experience in interior design and event planning, they can craft the perfect setting for your *Stay In* date. Check out their website at: *www.by-michelle.com*

D. Fantasy List

Make her fantasy come true. Ask your amour to describe her favorite feasible fantasy and then reveal that you are going to plan an evening around that fantasy and make it a reality. Break down the elements of the evening and determine how best to create your girlfriend's fantasy. You will have a blast planning this!

Tips to remember:

- Set limits for the fantasy in terms of distance, location or budget. That is up to you.
- Make it something to look forward to and indulge each other's fantasy. Whether you verbalize it in bed, over dinner, or write a sexy note to each other with the details, it doesn't matter. The important key is that you share the fantasy and are comfortable sharing this and then decide on a time frame to carry them out!

6 Budget Dates ($ to $$ / ♥ to ♥♥)

You don't have to be a Rockefeller to date. If you have expendable cash and want to spend lots of dough wooing your lady love, then by all means do it. But, if your money strings are a bit shorter, you don't have to break the bank. The goal of dating is to find someone, get to know them, fall in love and then find out enough about them and who they are to know if you are meant to be with them for the rest of your life. It all comes down to chemistry and whether each of you possess the values and qualities that you are looking for in one another. We understand you may not want to appear cheap. But, that doesn't mean you can't be monetarily cautious. We get it! Do your goals and what you want in life and the kind of life you want match? If you are not sure and you are figuring it out — that's OK. You can still date to figure that out. The dates in this grouping are meant to be interesting, silly and affordable. Especially early on in a relationship where you want to get to know someone but not blow your savings on a girl you are not sure you want as your wife, then these dates are a good place to start.

DATE	COST	ROMANCE
Ice Skating and Hot Chocolate	$	♥♥♥
Pumpkin / Apple Picking and Hay Ride	$ - $$	♥♥♥
Picnic and Make-Out Point	$ - $$	♥♥♥
Bowling	$ - $$	♥♥
Flea Markets	$	♥♥
Garage Sales	$	♥
Political Lecture	$	♥
Driving Range	$	♥
Soup Kitchen	$	♥♥
Clean Your Car	$	♥♥
Art Gallery Tour	$	♥♥
Open Houses	$	♥
Poetry / Book Reading	$	♥♥
Religious Service and Brunch	$	♥
Visit Your Favorite TV Show	$	♥

Things to consider:
- These dates are mostly meant as a "get to know you" date that is affordable.
- It is a good date to do even if you are an established couple or married.
- These dates are very inexpensive. Sure, you can amp up the romance and the cost, but that is unnecessary.
- Very little planning is involved. Maybe a call or two and an internet search. They can even be considered spontaneous.

Things you may need:

Good conversation, sense of fun, newspaper (for house listings or flea market listings).

A. Ice Skating and Hot Chocolate

It's winter and ice-skating is a perfect venue to get close to your honey and swirl her around the ice rink. Ice-skating is festive and reminiscent of a more innocent and simpler time. Therefore, in keeping with that, why not go for hot chocolate afterward? You can keep your girl warm until you sit down to a hot cocoa with perhaps a hint of something sweet and sugary. She will be all smiles at what a fun day it was and, ... she will be right.

B. Pumpkin / Apple Picking and A Hayride

It's October and Halloween is approaching. Why not take a scenic drive to a farm where you can pick your own pumpkins or apples? While there, take a hayride and savor some hot apple cider. After a day in the brisk October air, head back to your place where you can order in and enjoy a light hearted contest to see who can carve the scariest face on a pumpkin. Add a little spice by making a wager on who wins what. A kiss perhaps? Again, a free-spirited time that is invigorating and affordable. It will be a sure-fire date that will have your lady gushing over how much fun she had with you that day!

C. Picnic and Make Out Point

We have suggested a lot of picnics throughout the various date suggestions in this book. Sometimes, they just fit in great with the plans of the day.

Sharon can never think of a picnic that doesn't include a fun high school style make out session. Isn't that innocently sexy? If you are not into PDAs, (public displays of attention) then have a great picnic and on the way home, find a quiet spot with a view where you can pull the car over and enjoy. While you are soaking in the view, you can decide to give your lady love a kiss – and another kiss – and another kiss. It may take some work finding what we call a "make out point." We have confidence that you will find it or keep your eye out for one. For example, in New York, there is a scenic pull off the highway for views of the Hudson that are very private. So pull off that road, enjoy a great view and — well, you can take it from here!

D. Bowling

Bowling is just an unadulterated good time out. As long as you don't have tennis elbow, this is an all American good night out as a couple or on a double date. It is Americana to us and is an activity that binds people of all ages and backgrounds for their one common love of trying to get 10 pins down with one throw of a ball. The competitive aspect of the activity can also be enticing. So, go put on shoes you would never wear otherwise, pick a lane and a ball, and have a blast trying to get a strike. Funny how a strike in one sport is great (bowling) and yet in another (baseball) it's a bad thing. Ah, what is a girl to do to understand sports? Well, you can help her figure it out. Maybe your lady has never bowled before, which is unimaginable we know, so you have the added advantage of being able to stand close to her and show her how to throw the ball. We know you won't strike out — wait, that's a baseball reference — sorry, wrong sport!

E. Flea Markets

Talk about an affordable and lazy afternoon. There are many great flea markets where you can score amazing deals. Do you or your sweetie love a bargain? This is a perfect opportunity to survey the goods and even bargain if you feel up to the challenge. If you decide to get your lady a memento, it will probably cost you less than $5. Entrances to most flea markets are free. So, if you are looking for an afternoon that is affordable to you and has shopping for her, then what could be a more perfect day? They are easy enough to find through the internet or local papers. Go find a flea market and suggest an afternoon of it to your gal — trust us, she will say yes.

F. Garage Sales

Garage sales are all the rage. Spring and summer tend to be garage sale season and it is a wonderful way to spend a Saturday or Sunday afternoon. Some garage sales have pure junk, and yet others have real deals. Something you are looking for? Enjoy the negotiation. Maybe you can play *bad* cop to her *good* cop. If you have an eye for things of value and see an item that could be worth way more than the price tag – still try for a lower price. Even if you have to pay full price, hopefully your sense of value will pay off. We find garage sales are a good place to find jewelry, glassware or housewares at a much discounted price. It may not be something you do every weekend, but it sure is an entertaining way to spend an afternoon. Also, the people-watching at garage sales is priceless!

G. Political Lecture

Are you or your lady political junkies? Even if you are not on the same ticket with your politics that doesn't mean you can't enjoy them, debate them successfully or hear varying views. If you don't belong to a political group, you may want to. It will give you exposure to interesting guest lectures in your area at different venues. They could be in the form of a debate or a guest speaker or a panel of speakers with varying views on politics or specific issues. Either way, it will be a stimulating and informative evening that can spark some interesting exchanges. You can also check the internet or your local paper. Many colleges host such events at their campuses or their School Alumni Clubs (in major cities). We have seen some fascinating debates and wonderful speakers who gave us unexpected food for thought.

H. Driving Range

Golf is a popular sport and something that you can do as a couple. Regardless of what level of experience either of you have, the driving range is fun and you can take it as seriously or as silly as you want to. If you are really good at golf, what better way to get up close and personal with the girl who makes your heart flutter than standing behind her showing her how to grasp and swing a golf club. It is outdoorsy without feeling like the Olympics, and she doesn't have to worry about perspiring too much (yes, we do think of those things). It won't take too long, so if you are bored, you can split afterwards. If you are having fun and want to get to know her better, then ask her for a bite to eat afterward. Either way, we think you will both enjoy the driving range!

I. Soup Kitchen / Homeless Shelter

If you are both active in volunteerism and believe in helping your fellow human when you can, then this might be the perfect venue to get to know each other and do something good at the same time. There are many soup kitchens that need help cooking and serving to those in need. Find one associated with a church or charity (if you are not affiliated with one already) and volunteer together. You can really see each other's soul and observe how she interacts with others. Even if she is not for you, at least you will have helped another person. This will be one of the most rewarding dates you will ever have! For example, Habitat For Humanity is great for the handyman or woman who wants to give back to the community. Or, volunteer at the Special Olympics. You can also raise money doing a walk for March of Dimes Walk or Cure for Breast Cancer.

J. Clean Your Car

OK, so neither of us necessarily consider this a *date*. It is more like a casual get-together that could lead to dating or is an activity that, as you really get to know someone, you will agree to just because you want to spend more time with them. But, maybe you really need your car cleaned and you can kill two birds with one stone. Yes, we can see how this date can get frisky once you involve suds and water. Sure, it will start out innocent, but once that first splash or spray is sent, then it can be a free for all of silliness where you can be all cute and touchy-feely. Wait a minute; maybe this really is a good date idea after all!

K. Art Gallery Tour

Art galleries are free to roam around in, so why not go to an "arty" section of town and stroll from gallery to gallery admiring the work of local and international artists. You can have fun pretending that you are rich yuppies looking to find that "perfect" painting with a "flair of innocence combined with the complexity of passion." In the art world you can say things like that with conviction – things that don't make sense but sound really deep and intellectual. Just don't giggle when you do this and give yourself away. You can laugh once you get back out on the street. And who knows, you may actually find something that resonates with both of you. Once you have twirled around all the paintings you can't afford, you can always do something that is affordable such as go for a drink and talk about what you did see. It doesn't matter whether your chats are serious or silly, because what is important is that you are spending time together learning about each other.

L. Open House

Mariann loved open houses so much she got her realtor's license. On a Sunday afternoon, go for brunch and then jump in the car and go check out neighborhoods that intrigue you. It's a great way to see what styles each of you like - and price range! You can really take a look at what things cost today or you can do what Mariann likes to do when she's in Los Angeles. She visits expensive open houses and tells them she just got a production deal and the house at two million is nice, but her range is really three million and she's looking for something bigger. It's a carefree way to spend an afternoon.

M. Poetry / Book Reading

If you or your gal have a literary side or a favorite author, what is better than going to a bookstore for a reading by that author? Bookstores are dwindling, but there are always select chain locations or local book stores that will promote a stimulating speaker series or spotlight an author. Whether it is a poetry reading or book reading, it is a blast to meet the author and mingle with people who love words and books as much as you do. Also, there are literary societies you can join. Or, if you join an ethnic group they too can host readings. For example, the Irish Historical Society in New York City or the Glucksman Ireland House connected with NYU (New York University) have programs that are Irish based in music, writing, poetry and history. All interesting events that are free or affordable that appeal to what interests you. If you are both wordsmiths, then you will be guaranteed a great date! Check out your local cultural or historical societies or universities.

N. Religious Service and Brunch

Do you both have a religious conviction that you share? That is great. If you do, then perhaps you can attend a service together and then go for breakfast or a bite afterward. It's nice to know that you share something important to you and that you can both express that. This is a sweet date that will mean a lot to her if you both share in and respect your religious affiliation, whatever that is!

O. Visit Your Favorite TV Show

Imagine sitting 100 feet away from your favorite comedian or talk show host. It is possible. And, it's free. Just pick a show you both love and send for tickets. Whether you are in New York City or Los Angeles, there are great shows to see like Ellen, The David Letterman Show, The Chew, The Talk, Jimmy Fallon to name just a few. Afterward go for dinner or be on the lookout for other celebrities at some unassuming restaurant or bar in a cool part of town. Either way, this date will score high with both of you!

7 Day Excursions ($ to $$$ / ♥ to ♥♥♥)

Day trips can tell you a lot about someone. Are they fun? Moody? Demanding? Easy Going? With a day trip, you can determine if you can take this person for a longer period of time than an average four-hour date. You have more time to talk and really get to know the person or explore issues or topics that perhaps a movie night does not offer. Does the person make the day go faster because you are enjoying her company so much? Is she demanding and realize this is something you never saw in her before? Does she go from Dr. Jekyll to Ms. Hyde with her mood swings? If something goes wrong is she accepting or supportive or a whiny bitch? Is she always upbeat and happy? By the end of the day, I think you will have a clearer picture of the person you are dating.

DATE	COST	ROMANCE
Antiquing	$ - $$$	♥♥♥
Wine Tasting Tour	$ - $$	♥♥♥
Music Festivals	$ - $$$	♥♥
Zoo	$ - $$	♥
Caverns	$	♥♥
Historical Villages	$ - $$	♥♥
Whale Watching	$ - $$	♥♥
Civil War Re-Enactments	$	♥
Under the Big Top	$ - $$$	♥♥
Casino – Let It Ride	$ - $$$	♥♥
Beer Crafting and Breweries	$ - $$	♥♥

Things to consider:

- These dates are meant to be relaxing and low stress so you and your girlfriend, whether she is new or a long-standing flame, can be together, talk and enjoy.
- These dates are not expensive and yet shake things up from the boring "let's just go to dinner" date.
- These dates appeal to a lot of different interests. Not sure if you would enjoy a Civil War re-enactment? Try it to find out.

- Find events in the local papers or the internet or regional magazines.
- You can make them as romantic as you want.

Things you will need:
Picnic basket/blanket/food, willingness to try something different.

A few years ago Mariann was dating someone who she thought she could go the distance with and heard distant wedding bells in her future. One day they took a day trip and got to talking about his hobbies and career. Over the course of the day, Mariann found his conversation laced with a lot of condescension and pompousness she had never seen on shorter dates. It was disappointing to her. As he was talking, she thought to myself, "can I listen to this for the rest of my life?" The answer, sadly, was "NO."

As you can see, these day trips can divulge a lot. You can also come away from a day-long date thankful because it was so enjoyable and be awed at how time flew, what a good time you had and how much you laughed. You may realize you both have a lot of simpatico. Listen to her and your instincts. Most importantly, listen to what is being said between the lines!

A. Antiquing

Take a day and explore antique shops where you can find hidden treasures that will appeal to you both. Regardless of whether it is glassware, jewelry, furniture or some cool metalwork you find that is intriguing and you're interested in buying, the goal of the day is to have a wonderful experience with your favorite lady. If you're not in a buying mood, just window shop. Either way it will be a casual and low stress day. Start the day early with a light breakfast, then find an antique trail in your area. For example, if you live in the Northeastern United States, there are plenty of trails where you can find eclectic places that sell items that were popular in years gone by. Find a quaint café and relax as you take a look at the antique map or figure out where to go next. Enjoy a relaxing car ride listening to music and talking about your new purchases. The day will stroll by quickly as you both enjoy uninterrupted quality time together. If you are both serious antiques fans, you can make a weekend of visiting shops along a trail. It's a nice tranquil getaway!

Suggestions and information:

- If you live in the southeast, here is one antique trail for those states: *www.antiquetrail.com/*
- Here is a list of antique stores by state: *www.usa-antiquestores.com/*
- For a list of antique shows and fairs: *www.antiquetheusa.com/*
- Looking for an antique dealer? Here ya go: *www.usantiquedealer.com/*
- A list of antique stores and dealers across the USA: *antiquesacrosstheus.com/*
- If you Google/Yahoo "antique trail" and your location, you will find on antique trails with a concentration of stores in your area.

If you really want to surprise your girl or show her that you were listening, then perhaps you buy something she was looking at and really liked but decided not to buy and then give it to her for a birthday, holiday or as a "just because" gift. It will be a memorable date and a thoughtful gesture!

B. Wine Tasting Tour

Wine Tasting is a great outing as a couple or as a group. There are surprisingly a lot of wine trails throughout the country. Look up the wineries and wine trails in your area. You can go by yourselves or there may be buses sponsored by the wineries that take people wine tasting. If you want to go in style, then arrange a limo or car service so you are safe on the roads and can both imbibe!

Tips to remember:

- Don't get sloppy drunk.
- If you want to class up the date and have the funds, get a limo or car service.
- Make sure to check out the wine trails and logistically plan which winery you will begin and end with.
- Make sure to eat (picnic or at the winery) before you start wine tasting.
- Some wineries serve food or can arrange a picnic basket for you in advance (you will have to call). If not, pack your own picnic lunch, cuddle up and enjoy. How romantic!
- Pick one winery where you can find a romantic or pretty spot, throw down a blanket and split a bottle of the wine you just purchased

together. If it has been a while since lunch, then most wineries sell cheese and crackers. We usually like the winery where we relax and enjoy a bottle of wine to be the last one, but that is up to you.

- We would not recommend more than 3 wineries in an afternoon. Otherwise, you might feel rushed.
- Some wineries have bands too. So, be aware of the amenities of the wineries you visit.

Suggestions and information:

- Here are a few links that spotlight wine trails throughout the USA:
  > *americaswinetrails.com/*
  > *www.winetrailsusa.com/*
- Just Google/Yahoo "wine trail" and your location for a listing.

The effects of the grape will tear down any nervousness or shyness and your buzz will have you feeling happy and silly. When your defenses are down, it's easier to bond and get to know each other. Please do be careful not to get so drunk that you can't walk or get sick as that may just be your last date. This is a great way to spend a day but please *do* make sure that neither of you tastes so much wine that you can't drive. If your budget allows, hiring a car and driver for the day would be a good idea.

C. Music Festivals

Come spring and summer, Music Festivals abound. You can make a good 'ole country day of it by packing up the car with a huge blanket, some snacks and a positive attitude and taking a drive through pretty countryside to attend a music festival. Listen to an array of bands and you may be surprised to find yourself the newest groupie of a band you've come love. Extend the trip and make it an overnight adventure. If you both love music and being outdoors, then this date will sing of success.

Suggestions and information:

- Here are a few links to check out that spotlight the various music festivals throughout the USA:
  > *www.thespacelab.tv/spaceLAB/theSHOW/Spacelab-MusicFestivals.htm*
  > *musicusafestivals.org/*

> *www.festivals.com/*
> *www.festivalfinder.com/*
> *www.festivals-and-shows.com/music-festivals.html*

If you search music festivals and your location, events will be listed. You can always check out a few bands you like and see if they are giving a free outdoor concert.

D. Zoo

Neither of us had been to a zoo in years and last year Mariann went on a date to the Bronx Zoo in New York City. She had an unexpectedly fabulous time. It was so refreshing to walk around a zoo and look at all the magnificent animals that live below the water and on the land. Even the petting portion of the zoo was joyous. Mariann is a Taurus – a bull. So, she was really touched when her date bought her a cute stuffed bull. Feeding the animals was a treat and it was awesome to be outdoors and walking around with so many different kinds of animals within arm's reach! Who could hate watching animals at a zoo? Trust us, she'll enjoy it!

Suggestions and information:
• Here are a few links that list the zoos throughout the USA: *www.officialusa.com/stateguides/zoos/*
• For the list of top Zoos, here is a good link: *www.unitedstatestouristattractions.com content/top_zoos_in_the_united_ states.html*

E. Caverns

Caverns? I know what you are thinking. Caverns? Yes. Now, your area may not have caverns, but if they do or are within driving distance, it's an intriguing and unusual destination for a date. Many caverns are long and deep enough to have tours that take you underground to see the earth from a different perspective. Have a nice lunch or pack a picnic. Take the scenic route there and just enjoy soaking in the view and visiting a sight you would *not* normally gravitate to. You will never be accused of not having new ideas or originality!

Suggestions and information:
- Here are a few links that list caverns and caves:
  > *cavern.com/*
  > *www.touristinformationdirectory.com/cave/list_of_caves.htm*
  > *www.showcaves.com/english/usa/region/ByRegion.html*

F. Historical Villages

There are many historical towns or villages scattered around this nation. Take a look and see if one is near you. They can vary from just a quaint shopping village to an Olde Village with activities and shops and sights that are reflective of early America. Even the Amish section of Pennsylvania is fascinating because you can tour a working farm and see how the Amish live. If you are in the mood for chocolate, Hershey Park in eastern Pennsylvania is a delicious destination with rides, tours and all things chocolate.

Suggestions and information:
- If you are in New England, here is a listing for historical villages and seaports: *www.antiquing.com/historic.htm*
- Here is a link to the National Park Service for park and historical info: *www.cr.nps.gov/nr/*
- Near Virginia? Try beautiful Williamsburg: *www.colonialwilliamsburg.com/*
- If you are in New Jersey, there is Allaire Village, Batsto Village and Smithville:
  > *allairevillage.org/*
  > *batstovillage.org/*
  > *www.historicsmithvillenj.com/*

New Jersey has a History Fair in the summer which can be unique and interesting to attend. Other states have tours or interactive activities and most always have a General Store. Hey, a girls gotta shop ya know! Talk about a great way to wander around hand in hand in warm weather having a fun day all the while learning a little history in between.

G. Whale Watching

Mariann always thought whale watching was boring. But as she learned, it's not. Watching these magnificent animals spring up out of the water and gracefully twist their huge bodies is an unbelievable sight. And if you see a group of them do it at once, it is like watching a water ballet. You never know where you will see them but what a beautiful way to spend an afternoon. Sometimes the boats have snacks and you can grab a soda or a glass of wine and let your hair blow in the wind as the boat moves along with the waves towards shore! Obviously, you have to be on the East or West coast. Sorry Nebraska! We've have gone in Cape Cod, near Provincetown. Afterward, we stopped by a restaurant on the water and had a fabulous lobster dinner. Talk about being content and happy. Your date will be too. OK, so if she hates boats and the water and she's very prone to sea sickness, you might want to choose from one of the other dates!

H. Civil War Re-Enactment

Sharon dated someone who was a history buff. He devoured anything about history whether it was a book or DVD or special program. If your date loves history or a specific time in days gone by, then take her to a museum that focuses on that time period. Sharon's guy loved the Civil War. While perusing the local paper, she saw there would be a Civil War re-enactment so she planned a day around that. He couldn't have been happier. Sharon was able to shop at the fair and he became enthralled watching the costumed actors holding minuteman rifles while replaying historical battles. Sharon's date was a happy boy, which made Sharon a happy girl.

Suggestions and information:

• Check your local or regional paper for events going on near you that might include a Civil War Re-enactment.
• Here are a few sights that list re-enactments around the country:
  > *reenactmenthq.com/*
  > *www.civilwartraveler.com/events/*

I. Under The Big Top

Another idea to consider is going to the Circus. Who doesn't love jugglers and clowns under the big top and elephants that can stand on two feet. It's fun and will propel you back to the innocence and fun of your childhood. This is also a great opportunity to delve deeper into each other's lives and childhoods. What better way to open up the subject of one another's youth and formative years than by starting with childhood circus memories? Grab your date and have a blast Under The Big Top!

J. Pub Crawl

Do you enjoy a drink and live in or near a city? Consider a *Pub Crawl* or *Literary Pub Crawl*. It has a theme and will take you to notable places where you can salute or toast the literary icons that have left us with the treasure of their words. You can set this up yourself or check your local or city paper or internet to find groups that have pub crawl tours. One of Sharon's fondest and most romantic date memories is stopping for drinks at The Algonquin in New York City with a guy she was crazy about. The Algonquin is where the writer Dorothy Parker met with the other literary powerhouses of her day at what became known as "The Algonquin Round Table". As a writer herself, the sheer romanticism and literary history of that place had her over the moon!

K. Casino — Let It Ride

Jump in the car and stop by the bank to cash in all the coins and pennies you saved in that jar – yes we know, all guys have that coin jar! Then head to a local casino. You've bet on love and seemed to have won, so why not try your luck at the tables or slot machines. Pool some money and play the machines together. Are you a crackerjack at cards? Then try 21. Or perhaps you hit the craps table where she'll be your lucky charm. Casinos have restaurants of all kinds from inexpensive and casual to upscale and pricey. If you win at the tables, then treat your gal to a good bottle of wine and a tasty meal. Not so lucky today? Hey, the buffalo wings at the diner are good too. You will get caught up in the exuberance of the lights and sounds and vibe of being a winner!

Suggestions and information:
• Here are two websites that list all the casinos and gambling outlets in the USA:
> *www.uscasinocity.com*
> *www.worldcasinodirectory.com*

L. Beer Crafting and Breweries

Independent and craft breweries are on the rise and all the rage. They are popping up all over the nation and if you do a little search, you will find these craft breweries near you. If you and your girl enjoy a few cold beers, then make a list and visit them one by one and discover your favorite. Some also have lessons in how to make beer. There are also beer festivals you can attend and if you want to make a long weekend out of, you'll have a great time sampling many beers.

Suggestions and information:

- Here is a website to learn about beer and small and independent breweries: *www.craftbeer.com*
- Looking for breweries by state? Try this site: *www.beerinfo.com*
- An association that promotes brewers is: *www.brewersassociation.org*
- Here is a site with top 10 beer festivals in the USA: *voices.yahoo.com/top-10-beer-festivals-united-states-4068635.html*
- The Top 10 biggest US Craft Breweries are: *www.cnbc.com/id/39233398/The_10_Biggest_US_Craft_Breweries*
- Learn how to make your own beer: *www.beercrafting.com*

8 Destination Date ($$$$$ / ♥♥♥♥♥)

The allure of a destination outside your home town is energizing and the anticipation alone builds great excitement. You can explore this adventure in a few ways.

DATE	COST	ROMANCE
A Night In The Tropics	$$$$$	♥♥♥♥♥
Big City Lights	$$$$$	♥♥♥♥♥
Baby, It's Cold Inside	$$$$$	♥♥♥♥♥

Things to consider:

• These dates are expensive, involve a lot of planning and are for those who are in very serious relationships who really want to *wow* your gal and treat her to something exceptional.

• You can tell your gal and plan the adventure together. Or, you can surprise your lady and advise her to take the time from work, pack her bags and expect an adventure.

• You have to do much research on the activities, sights and accommodations of your destination.

• Take the time to really plan a framework for the time away. Remember to leave some time for spontaneity and discovery — and some love making!

Things you may need:

Travel guides, air reservations, hotel reservations, mementos, love note, sexy gift bag.

A. A Night In The Tropics

It's time to take your sweetie to a new destination and spend some alone time together that is saucy with a bit of spice! Pick a warm place in the tropics where you can sun on the beach, tan on a boat, sip cocktails poolside or dine on succulent food. Interested in Snorkeling? Scuba Diving? Boating? Food? Spa? Whatever the activity, you will definitely be an "A" star rated boyfriend or fiancé if you find that breathtaking view in the tropics where you can go boating, be entertained and stimulate the senses.

Tips to remember:

- Make this a dream vacation for you and your lady. Has she been talking about needing a rest and wanting to sit under a palm tree sipping margaritas? If yes, this is the perfect vacation.
- There are several tropical destinations such as Cabo San Lucas in Mexico, The Dominican Republic, Fiji, Bermuda and Belize to name a few. Go on-line and see what deals you can get.
- Make your girlfriend feel like she is pampered. You are not her servant, but make her feel cared for and attended to. We know she will appreciate it.
- Really use this time to forget the outside world, relax and bond. Be tactile, affectionate, and loving. Have fun and just enjoy being a couple without a worry in the world.
- Turn off your cell phone. Let her know she's much more important than that message from work.

Suggestions and information:

- For good deals on air and hotel, go to Bloomspot *www.bloomspot.com*, Jetsetter *www.jetsetter.com*, Groupon *www.groupon.com*, or Travelzoo *www.travelzoo.com* to name a few.
- Some hotels are all inclusive, which means your room, meals, activities, and sometimes even alcohol, are all included in one price. This is a great option if you want to concentrate on vacationing with your date and not your wallet.

B. Big City Lights

Big cities are a vast playland of varying personalities and possibilities for amusement and romance. There is something for every taste and desire. Great restaurants. Cultural sites. Beautiful scenery. Historical attractions. Shopping. Theater. Comedy. Sex shops. Iconic music venues and great views. You can either plan a surprise trip away or make it a cooperative effort with your lady love having final approval. If she is a woman in control, then this may be your best bet. First you need to find out that one destination big city she has always wanted to visit or go back to. If it's a surprise, give her enough information so she can be prepared with clothes and vacation time. To build the suspense you can send her notes, cards or trinkets that give hints or are romantic stating how much you can't wait to be away on your adventure. If you just want to surprise her with the idea and then plan your trip together, take her to a restaurant or venue that has the cuisine or vibe that best represents where you are going. Then, wrap up a symbol of that city in a box and have her open it. Inside you can write on a card or a scroll with details about your destination. The symbol does not have to be expensive unless you want it to be. It is just that — a symbol.

Tips to remember:
- **What to do?** – Ask yourself what your girlfriend *loves* to do? What excites her? Is there something that moves her?
- **Shopping** – Every city has a shopping district or areas that suit different styles or host many designers. Find out what areas are in your destination city. It's fun to window shop. You will adore the view when she tries on that *little black dress*. Better yet, make one of those sexy little dresses a gift for her.
- **Dining** – Most big cities host some of the best and most eclectic cuisine. What does your lady like? Five star? Vegan? Chic? Steakhouse? View? If you've been *listening* to your lady, you should know her culinary tastes — this is your chance to impress her. Perhaps you find a cozy bohemian themed Tapas place perfect to stare into each other's eyes and fall in love all over again.
- **Destination Ambience** – What kind of adventure do you want to have? Do you want to wing it or have it more structured? What kind of ambience do you want in your hotel or restaurants? These are things you need to think about. If you want grand and traditional or chic and modern, you will find it. You just need to know what it is you want.
- **A Never Ending Night** – Big cities are open late. You can find something to do at any hour. Determine what kinds of nights you want to share. Perhaps you want a spot for salsa or ballroom dancing or a loud club where the thumping of the base gets you fired up on the dance floor. Or, you want an elegant champagne bar where you can pretend to be famous movie stars from the 20's. Maybe a rooftop bar that provides stunning views of the many city lights. We live outside New York City and can advise on all things New York. For example, there is a place in New York City called *Milk And Honey*. It's fashioned after an old speakeasy and they don't give you a drink menu. You tell

them what you like and they will customize or determine the drink to give you. It's dark and cozy enough to snuggle in the booth and feel as if you have taken a step back in time to an era of prohibition where you wouldn't even be allowed to drink. Try your hotel piano bar and if they don't have one, go to a piano bar like the Monkey Bar which is a tiny place with good drinks, food and music! And, if you want to end the evening with a romantic carriage ride in Central Park, you don't have to go far. Again, rely not only on your concierge but the internet as an excellent source to check things out. You can always visit the travel section at your local bookstore.

- **Music** – Cities offer a vast array of musical venues and styles that appeal to people of all ages and backgrounds from 18 to 80. So, whatever you like whether it is progressive, rap, country, folk, R & B, rock, Broadway, cabaret or jazz, you will find it in a big city. Jazz just puts Mariann into a zen zone and Broadway music keeps her humming for hours afterward. Cabaret music makes her think she should have been born decades before she was. Sharon loves rock and country makes her tap her feet and R & B – well that just makes her head bob back and forth. Plan a night where music is what scores your evening!

- **Theater** – Theatrical productions abound in big cities from one man shows, to experimental presentations at little theaters to major plays and grand musicals. Again, if your lady loves theater and acting, plan an evening with that as the focal point.

- **Dance and Classical Music** – Whether your date loves ballet or modern dance, there are plenty of dance companies and opera houses and symphonies that will give her what she craves.

- **Museums** – Big cities love their museums. Be it art, natural history, science or unusual ethnic or interactive experience, find one where you can relax as you slowly stroll the many exhibits.

- **Create a Memory** – This is really important. It does not have to be expensive but it does have to be meaningful. Gift your girlfriend with something that commemorates your special moment or this journey to *the Big City*. From a crystal ornament to a refrigerator magnet of an iconic building to a print of her favorite artist's work or a CD of the musical you just saw, let her know you want to remember this time together. It's not about the price, it's about the acknowledgment and celebration of her and your time and experience together.

We strongly recommend that you contact the concierge at the hotel of your destination and work with them (if you need it) on ideas, planning and logistics. That is what they are there for. Just be sure to acknowledge their efforts with a tip ($20-$50) depending on the level of assistance. If this is not a surprise and your gal knows about the trip, then perhaps you can plan it together but keep a few surprises or fun elements to yourself until you experience them together.

End the trip with a card that she can read the last night of your getaway or in the plane or car on the way home. Be honest and tell her how much you enjoyed seeing her eyes light up or loved hearing her laugh or seeing her feet tap to the music she loved so much. Tell her how she made you feel. Or, that she was stunning in that sexy dress and took your breath away. Whatever the content of your note, be honest and have it come from the heart. She will keep it forever and even when you don't know it, she will go back and re-read it time and again.

C. Baby, It's Cold Inside

Take your originality off the charts and go really, really different. Now, if your lady *hates* the cold, you may want to skip this date and go to the Tropics. But, if she likes adventure and the cold, then take her on a once in a lifetime trip — an Ice Hotel. They have them in Canada, Norway, and Sweden. In Canada there is an annual Ice Hotel about 20 minutes north of Quebec City and an Ice Village with rooms and restaurants just outside of Montreal. In Sweden, you can mix it with a trip to see the Northern Lights by snowmobile and then have dinner at a restaurant with cuisine made from local ingredients. After a night in the Ice Hotel, move to a chalet in the montains or visit a nearby city.

An Ice Hotel takes a year to build and it is *art*. They're crafted by teams of over 300 international artists. Even as the website (www.icehotel.com) quotes: *"The hotel's snow corridors are tunnels of adventure in which each suite opens the door to a whole new world. It is spellbinding and surrealistic."* Please know these are *not* hotels where you go and stay for five nights. You stay for a night, or two if you adore the cold. Then you go to a nearby chalet with heat. Just imagine, unwinding at the end of the evening in the ICE BAR and snuggling under the thermal sleeping bags in your hotel room.

Tips to remember:

- Make sure you have your passport.
- Make reservations at the heated chalet after your night in the Ice Hotel and have the hotel arrange the snowmobiling to experience the northern lights.
- Bring layers of clothing to accommodate the level of cold you feel.
- Make sure this is an experience she would love!

Suggestions and information:

- Check out the features of the Ice Hotel at *www.icehotel.com*
- Don't want to go to Europe? They have an ice hotel in Canada too: *www.hoteldeglace-canada.com/*.
- You'll find Montreal's Ice Hotel at the annual Snow Village at *www.snowvillagecanada.com/*

We're not going to make a corny joke about the heat of your love melting the ice. Nope, not gonna do it. Too easy to go there! We guarantee you this will be a trip and *chilling time* you will never forget.

9 Different Is Good ($ to $$$$ / ♥♥ to ♥♥♥♥)

It's good to mix it up and do things that you wouldn't normally do or are outside your comfort zone. Is your date shy? Are you? Maybe a night out where you have to put your extrovert suit on might prove entertaining.

DATE	COST	ROMANCE
Dining and Dancing In The Dark	$ - $$$	♥♥♥♥
Karaoke – Gotta Sing!	$ - $$	♥♥
Letters Of The Alphabet	$ - $$$	♥♥
Space Camp	$$$ - $$$$$	♥♥♥

Things to consider:
- These dates can range from relaxing and recharging and G rated right up to hot and sexy and X rated.
- These dates don't require too much advanced planning. You may have to buy a few things in advance, but nothing you can't do on-line or go to the store for!
- Play up the romance and sense of fun.

Things you may need:

List of music and karaoke venues, some planning, originality, openness to new experiences, air and hotel reservations, event reservations, love notes, wine, cheese, bubble bath, candles.

A. Dining and Dancing In The Dark

They say that when you are in the darkness your other senses get heightened. Think back to how you feel when the lights go out and you're suddenly thrust into the darkness. Your pulse races, your smell and touch are heightened and there is a sense of excitement about the unknown. Apply that same philosophy to dining and you can understand the increasing popularity of restaurants offering "Dining in the Dark." At the restaurant, you are seated and served and eat in the dark where your sense of touch and taste are intensified.

Tips to remember:

- Make sure this is an experience your girlfriend will like. If she is a control freak or a picky eater, it may not be for her.
- Check out the venue to ensure it is a reputable restaurant offering this experience.
- This is definitely an experience outside the norm. Just enjoy it!
- Be conscious of the fact that many of the waiters are blind since they don't need to see.
- These restaurants tend to just be in the major cities.

I think this is an innovative concept that is a heightened sensory experience. This date is all about enjoying enjoying a different dining experience outside the norm where every course and bite holds suspense.

Suggestions and information:

- Google *Dining In The Dark* and your or location for options.
- This place in New York City has masks you wear while eating: *www.camaje.com/specialevents.html*
- This place holds events in New York, California and Texas. Try the Santa Monica, CA location: *la.darkdining.com/*
- In New York City, this place has events for dining in the dark: *newyork.danslenoir.com/*

Keep the theme of the night when you get back to your place. Turn off all the lights, play some music and slow dance ... *in the dark*. No candles. No lights. Close your shades and continue the experience. If you want to continue heightening your sense of touch, by all means, you may just want to take it into the bedroom.

B. Karaoke — Gotta Sing!

For years, Mariann studied vocally and concentrated on classical music and yet the thought of singing in front of a group scares the stuffing out of her. Music and singing are electrifying. How many times have you found yourself singing along to your favorite music in your car. Well, why not join a bunch of other people who love music and who mostly can't sing but have a great time trying. Karaoke is not about great singing. It is about having a great time. Do you or your gal have a favorite song you have always wanted to sing together? Ever wanted to do an open-mic night? Well, now is your chance. Go mingle with strangers, have a few drinks and let loose on the microphone.

Tips to remember:
- This is an inexpensive date so you can to let your hair own and just have a great time among a funny mix of people.
- Make sure your date is not so shy that she will feel uncomfortable.

Suggestions and information:
- Be careful of how much you drink. If in doubt, get a cab.
- Want to avoid a horrible hangover? Try the Mercy drink. It lessens the effects of alcohol. Take a drink before, a drink during and a drink after. We can attest it works! *www.drinkmercy.com*. Again, when in doubt, call a cab, or arrange for a car service for the evening!

C. Letters Of The Alphabet

A friend told us about this and we thought it was an adorable idea. You take a letter of the alphabet (might be a good idea to start with A and end with Z) and then you go on a date with things relating to that letter. You can both plan an outing together or you can each pick a letter and are then responsible for planning the date around that letter. Or, let your favorite lady pick a letter and you are responsible to organize the date. For example, If you pick the letter "C" it could revolve around places, food, activities or things beginning with "C". For example, Chinese food, Cigar Bar, Culture, and Cheese. Maybe you have a "Candlelight" dinner eating Chicken in a town or restaurant that begins with "C" after you going Canoeing with your Cutie." Well, you get the idea.

Tips to remember:
- This is meant to be a fun date that inspires your imagination. It can be as sweet or romantic as you like. Just dating? Make the date fun. Dating for a while? Use it to infuse joy and romance into your relationship.
- This does not have to be an expensive outing. It can be as economical or as luxurious as you want it to be.

D. Space Camp

We know this sounds like an unusual date or excursion, but it is *different*. Now, if you lady is not into flights, planes, space or astronauts, then this is not the date for her. If her inner nerd is in full gear, then Space Camp could prove to be one of the most clever dates you plan.

Tips to remember:

- This date runs a weekend and involves travel. It could involve air travel depending on where you live. It is best to go when you are in a committed relationship.
- Since travel is involved and the Space Camp charges a fee, the cost of this will be substantial. The course costs alone run a bit under $600 each. This is also a fun event to do with a group of your friends and you can all be on the mission together!
- The camp has a simulator. If your gal is prone to motion sickness or does not handle such things well, you might want to forego this date.
- You can suggest it and plan the outing together (or with a group of your friends), or you can surprise her – that is up to you.
- You should know beforehand if this date / weekend away would resonate with your girlfriend!

Mariann loves aviation and space. If she were dating a guy and he knew of her love for space and thought of this date or listened to her conversations where she has said repeatedly, "I really want to go to Space Camp" and arranged this, she would be on cloud 9. Space Camp (www.spacecamp.com) is out of this world … sort of! Per the website, "Adult Space Academy® is an adventurous two-night experience where trainees take roles in hands-on, interactive space mission and learn what it's like to train as an astronaut!"

Suggestions and information:

- Here are some links to Space Camp: *www.spacecamp.com/*
- Kennedy Space Center has an adult space camp: *www.spacecamp.com/adult.*
  Here is some other info on their site that might be helpful: *www.nasa.gov/centers/kennedy/about/information/camp_faq.html*
- And, they have other experiences that your nerdy gal may like: *www.kennedyspacecenter.com/program-inquiry.aspx*

Oh My God, doesn't that sound so cool and exhilarating? Yes, Mariann is letting her true inner geek come out and prance around like a nerd! She admits it. But, it would be a very different, typically once in a lifetime type experiences that will never be forgotten. If your girlfriend does not want to go — ask Mariann! She'll go.

10 For The Love Of Museums
($ to $$ / ♥ to ♥♥♥)

If your gal has a thirst for learning, culture and new experiences, then make a list of nearby museums and one by one spend a day soaking up all kinds of facts and folklore. There are museums dedicated to almost any interest under the sun. For a tranquil afternoon together that won't suck your bank account dry, this is the date for you.

DATE	COST	ROMANCE
Planetarium	$ - $$	♥
Museum Of Sex	$ - $$	♥♥♥
Tenement / Ethnic / Native American Museums	$ - $$	♥
Museum Of Natural History	$ - $$	♥
Art Museum	$ - $$	♥♥
Air and Space Museum	$ - $$	♥
Spy Museum	$ - $$	♥♥
Wax Museum / Ripley's Believe It Or Not	$ - $$	♥
Aquarium	$ - $$	♥♥

Things to consider:
- These dates are economical and can be done at any point in a relationship.
- You can make this a low key *get to know you* date or a really romantic outing.
- These dates stimulate intellect and interests that will bond you together.
- Want to keep the date going? Ask her to lunch or dinner.
- You can certainly check your local paper or internet for these and other museums in your area.

Things you will need:

Interest in what museum you are visiting, rose, relaxed attitude – don't appear bored or as if you are rushing her out the museum door.

A. Planetarium

We promise the planetarium can be a mind blowing experience. It is astounding when you realize who we are relative to the earth and who the earth is relative to the galaxy and that we are but just one galaxy in the universe. The planetarium is a such a fascinating, low key date that is awesome, interesting and affordable it will leave you *star* struck. It gives you something to talk about. Most planetariums have great shows that are incredibly thought provoking. Whether you and your gal are science-geeks or not, this can be a really interesting date. If you are really feeling a good vibe while sitting in the dark looking up at the sparkling stars watching the show, then just gently take her hand in yours.

Suggestions and information:
- Wikipedia has a good listing of Planetariums globally: *en.wikipedia.org/wiki/List_of_planetariums*
- Here is a good link to Planetariums located around the USA: *www.touristinformationdirectory.com/Planetarium/Science_Center_ Observatory_planetariums_US.htm*

B. Museum Of Sex

It's not just for nymphomaniacs. Is your lady friend interested in sex, the history of sex or anything about sex? Well if she is and loves a museum, then take her to the Museum of Sex. We will advise this is *not* a first, second or third date. We recommend not going to this museum until you know each other very well. These museums are in very specific locations such as New York City, Miami Beach and Las Vegas. If you are in Europe, you will find some variations in Paris, Russia, Copenhagen, Barcelona, Lithuania, London and Athens.

Tips to remember:
- Only go to this museum if you know your girl will not find it offensive nor take it as a hidden meaning to say that you want to have sex with her (yes, we know you do).
- This can be incorporated into your "Sexy Shopping" date if you want.

Suggestions and information:

- Some links for museums are: New York - *www.museumofsex.com/*
  This location has the first ever food-art-sex-cocktail bar! A great way to extend this spicy date.
- In Las Vegas - *www.eroticheritagemuseumlasvegas.com/*
- Wikipedia has the listings of such museums globally:
  en.wikipedia.org/wiki/Sex_museum#cite_note-3

You may not be able to go for a cold shower immediately following, but perhaps a cold beer or lemonade and a sugary delight! It will be a titillating afternoon where one or both of you may blush. I would consider this date as foreplay.

C. Tenement / Ethnic / Native American Museums

Many people like to learn more about their history and where they came from. Most major cities have ethnic or religious specific museums that may highlight or shed new light on your ancestry or religion. It will be inspiring and informative. For example, New York City has the Tenement Museum which is located downtown and they have different tours that highlight the various experiences of immigrants. Check out their website and find out what interests you. It will be an informative afternoon that once again can be appealing and low cost. If the date is going great, then just extend it by the invitation of dinner, drinks or coffee. That is up to you!

Suggestions and information:

- Here is a link of all Federal U.S. museums:
  www.usa.gov/Citizen/Topics/History-Museums.shtml

D. Museum Of Natural History

Fans of Jurassic Park and who love to know who and what went before our own time here on earth will love this museum. It is a great atmosphere to wander the vast rooms checking out the art, artifacts and history of our earth and world. You can go on a date and learn something at the same time. Many museums also have short movies or presentations, so make sure to get there in time to attend them, if you are interested.

Suggestions and information:

- There are Natural History museums all over the country. Here are some links that list all the museums by state:

    > *paleo.cc/kpaleo/museums.htm*

    > *www.museumsusa.org/museums/*

E. Art Museum

They're not just for artists. Maybe your gal can only draw stick figures but has the soul of an artist. Well, take her to an art museum where she can view art from the great iconic paintings and sculptures from the past up to works from more modern and avant-garde artists. Whatever her taste, there will be an exhibit hall that will resonate with her. Whenever a woman feels she has connected with her soul, she is more open and this enhances communication, personality and emotions. If you are the guy to recognize that, then you will be the recipient of that open mind and heart. When you see art, don't be afraid to be honest in your opinion. Don't be negative or dismissive of it, but if you like a picture or artifact then say you do and why. Likewise, if you don't like something, that is OK. Exchanging what you both see in a picture or sculpture can prove insightful. Go and be enlightened. It will be an emotionally rewarding afternoon.

Suggestions and information:

- There are museums all over the country. Here are some links that list all the museums by state:

    > *www.artcyclopedia.com/museums-us.html*

    > *museumca.org*

    > *www.museumsusa.org/museums/*

- If you prefer a private tour and have the extra funds, hire someone who will take you on a private tour or customize one for you. In New York City, there is an outfit, Art Smart, that does this exactly. Visit their website at: *www.artsmart.com*

F. Air and Space Museum

Anyone who loves history and is in awe of how far we have come in air and space travel will fall hard for a museum whose theme is air and space. It is all about the spirit of this country and the commitment that if you dream it and work at it, then you can achieve it. We just love that message. Mariann is a bit of a geek and nerd, so any guy who takes her to one of these museums would score big points. They highlight technology and innovation and thinking outside the box and she loves those attributes. Be prepared to be amazed and awestruck. If your lady loves these things, then you can bond over an exhilarated stroll through this museum while your heads are in the clouds.

Tips to remember:

- There are an array of Air and Space museums around the country. So, if this is not a day trip for you, then consider making it a weekend adventure.
- If this type of date doesn't resonate with her, then choose another type of museum.

Suggestions and information:

- There are museums all over the country. Just type "Air and Space Museum" in your favorite search engine listings will come up. Here's a site that lists by state: *www.aero.com/museums/museums.htm*
- Here are a few that might interest you:
  > Washington, D.C. - *airandspace.si.edu/*
  > Virginia - *www.vasc.org/*
  > San Diego, CA - *sandiegoairandspace.org/*
  > Tuscon, AZ - *www.aero.com/museums/museums.htm*
  > Air Force Museum in OH - *www.nationalmuseum.af.mil/*
  > Tulsa, OK - *www.tulsaairandspacemuseum.org/index.php*
  > St. Louis, MO - *airandspacemuseum.org/*
  > McMinnville, OR - *www.evergreenmuseum.org/*
  > Wapakoneta, OH – *www.armstrongmuseum.org/*
  > New York City, NY - *intrepidmuseum.org/*

Now, if your gal is only interested in re-runs of "Sex In the City" and going to exhibits of dresses of the First Ladies, then she will most likely not favor this museum. But, through your conversations, you'll know if this is a good pick or not!

G. Spy Museum

They're not just for spies. We have to admit, we did not know this existed until seven years ago. There is one in Washington, DC and Sharon was enthralled within minutes of entering. Of course, Sharon being a person who loves spy and espionage themed movies and books, she was sort of in heaven here. But, it is amazing what she learned that she did not know. She went with her family but it is still a great date place. As per the website: "A unique feature of the museum is its controlled entry, where visitors are given 5 minutes to memorize details of one of 16 spy profiles they are to assume (fictitious name, age, place of birth, destination, and so forth) as their "cover" before they are allowed to proceed into the exhibit area. Each "cover" is subtly assigned a mission on the plaque bearing its details, but completion is not required."

The Spy Museum offers other interactive or adventure oriented activities such as:

Spy Museum – Interactive – Operation Spy

If you want something more interactive they also have Operation Spy. Per the website, "The museum also has an interactive exhibit called Operation Spy, where visitors assume the roles of covert agents and participate in a one-hour Hollywood-style spy simulation, in which they move from area to area and are faced with puzzles, tasks, motion simulators, sound effects, and video messages as they work through a mission involving the interception of a secret arms deal involving a nuclear device. This exhibition has a separate admission fee and separate entrance from the museum's permanent exhibit."

Spy Museum – Adventure Hunt – Spy In The City

If you want something more *adventure hunt* oriented, they also have Spy In The City. The website states, "the museum began a new interactive called "Spy in the City", where visitors are given a GPS-type device and tasked with finding "clues" near various landmarks in the area surrounding the museum, for the purposes of fulfilling a "mission" of obtaining the password for a secret weapon."

Tips to remember:

- If this Spy Museum is not close enough to you for a day trip, then make it an overnight "special mission." Keep it economical and find a hotel just outside the city.
- I would just have fun with this date. Do not make it a political debate on the morality of spying!

Suggestions and information:

- Here is the link to the Spy Museum: *www.spymuseum.org/*
- This is a thought provoking and entertaining museum. The spy gift store afterwards is a blast. Whether you are a geek or not, you will love this thrilling museum!

H. Wax Museum / Ripley's Believe It Or Not

A wax museum is not just for voyeurs of the absurd. OK, maybe it is. This is a causal and silly date. The wax museum is cool because of how amazingly life-like the wax figures are. Have fun with picture taking. Recently, one guy Sharon went with did funny poses next to the wax figures that were hysterical and *laugh out loud funny*. Wax museums can be found in NYC, San Antonio, Las Vegas as well as the Hollywood Wax Museum in Hollywood, CA, Branson, MO and Gatlinburg, TN. There are other wax museums in New Orleans and San Francisco.

Ripley's Believe It Or Not exhibits bizarre things and ever so strange items. Some of it is hard to believe — so the name of the museum is appropriate for sure. But, it's diverse and entertaining. There are sights that will make you laugh and cringe. But, it will be interesting. There are locations in 26 cities around the country. You can check out what they have and their locations on their site. For an afternoon date where you want to make the date longer if the chemistry is there, you can't find a crazier and more bizarre place to go.

Suggestions and information:

- For a listing of wax museums:
  dir.yahoo.com/arts/humanities/history/museums_and_memorials/wax_museu ms/?skw=listings+of+wax+museums+in+the+USA

- Madame Tussauds is a popular wax museum with multiple locations: *www.madametussauds.com/washington/*
- For information on Ripley's and their locations, check out their site: *www.ripleys.com*

I. Aquarium

Who doesn't have a soft spot for Nemo? The undersea world with its hierarchy in the food chains is full of so many kinds of fish that vary in color from monochromatic to stunningly vibrant. Be a voyeur into the world below the surface. This a stress free date that will keep you saying *amazing*. There are aquariums of all sizes all around the country. So, go find one near you and see if you can find Nemo!

Suggestions and information:

- For a listing of aquariums around the country, this link should help: *www.touristinformationdirectory.com/united_states/Aquariums/public_ aquarium.htm*

11 Go For The Gold
($ to $$$$$ / ♥♥♥♥ to ♥♥♥♥♥)

The goal for these dates is to sweep your love off her feet. This is when you go so above and beyond that she feels like she is in a dream, living someone else's life, or she is Cinderella being swept off her feet by Prince Charming. These are more pricey date options, but where possible, we offer some more affordable options.

DATE	COST	ROMANCE
Serenade With A View	$$ - $$$	♥♥♥
C'est La Vie	$$$$$	♥♥♥♥♥
Do It By Candlelight	$ - $$$	♥♥♥♥♥

Things to consider:

- These dates are ultra-romantic and for someone you want to sweep off her feet.
- These dates involves research, planning and logistics. They can be expensive.
- If this is going to be a surprise, you need to get her things packed and ensure personal availability and vacation time, if necessary.
- A clever excuse may be necessary to hide the real surprise.

Things you may need:

Dining Guide (Zagat or internet), air or hotel points, air or hotel reservation, music or dining venue reservations, memento for memory or nice gift (jewelry), love notes, cards to mail to build anticipation of date, sexy gift (lingerie), champagne, rose petals, preparations for dinner, setting for dinner, blanket, poetry book, massage oils, new terry cloth robe, bubble bath, candles.

A. Serenade With A View

When you eat dinner, do you want to look at a swamp? Or view the top of a building smattered with generators, A/C units and water towers? No, of course not! A pretty view is always romantic whether you are looking at a lake, the ocean, the colorful harbor in Hong Kong, the lake in Chicago or the Chrysler Building in New York City. The vast expanse of Central Park in New York would be nice too. What does your date like? Is she big city and loves overlooking a river and viewing a skyline? Does she want to see the rhythmic waves of the ocean washing over the beach? Find the finest restaurant from one with a sleek and elegant design to a rustic house with a warming fireplace and make sure you get a table with the best view. The service should be impeccable. If it has a jazz trio or a piano in the background — all the better.

Tips to remember:
- Pick a place you know your girlfriend would love. If she likes elegant and you like Irish pub, take her to an elegant restaurant.
- Does she love champagne? Then splurge on her!
- Want to give her a little gift? Go ahead. We suggest something that means something to her from pearls to costume earrings that are affordable but may be a color or style she loves. Or an item that represents something special between the two of you.
- If you want to make it more romantic, write her a card or note telling her how you feel or a poem, if you have the gift of poetry.
- Are you in a city? Check if they have a carriage ride and really make her feel like Cinderella riding in her coach.
- If you want to make the evening last, whisk her away to a cozy lounge for an after dinner drink or forego dessert at the restaurant and go to a dessert bar with couches and get comfortable.

Suggestions and information:
- Use sites such as *www.zagat.com* or *www.yelp.com* to help with restaurant selection and reviews.
- Sites like *www.goldstar.com* or *www.travelzoo.com* have discounts and 50% off on restaurants, trips and activities.

Can't afford a top restaurant with a view to die for? No problem, pack an elegant basket with real dishes and cutlery and crystal wine glasses. Pack a nice dinner and set up a huge blanket on the beach at sunset or on a rooftop garden — bring some candles or lanterns to create a warm glow — pop open the bubbly — and you will still have your dinner with a view.

B. C'est La Vie

Surprise her. Go to Paris for the weekend. Sip champagne, stroll the Champs Elycees, dine overlooking the Eiffel Tower and stroll the lantern-lit streets of Paris as you slip into a quaint wine bar for a night cap.

Tips to remember:

- This date takes planning. Make sure she has a current passport.
- Make sure you find a way to get her clothes and toiletries (her girlfriend can assist). Or plan a fake surprise locally to get her to pack.
- It's fun if you make it a surprise. No worries though if you have to tell her so she can arrange vacation time.
- If you tell her in advance, find a fun way to do this. A note included in with her croissant perhaps explaining the surprise. Or pick up a small Eiffel Tower and tell her she will be seeing it up close and personal!

Suggestions and information:

- It's great to check out a deal on *www.groupon.com* , *www.bloomspot.com*, *www.jetsetter.com* or *www.orbitz.com* or any number of discount and travel sites for last minute deals.
- Can't make it to the real Paris? Maybe Paris Hotel and Casino in Vegas or France at Epcot both are good stand-ins that will still be enjoyed.

C. Do It By Candlelight

This date is meant to be a very sensual and loving evening at your place. It's a more economical but no less effective way to sweep her off her feet! Plan a romantic evening at your place and start a week or two before sending little love notes or inexpensive trinkets of your love or symbols of shared experiences. Does she love horses? Get her a refrigerator magnet with horses. Does she love dogs? Get her a stuffed dog. Is she an avid reader? Send her a small book of love poems. What's most important is that you tell her how you feel. Or you can just send a card that states, *"You make me smile."* Or, *"I love the softness of your hair and the smooth touch of your skin."* Or, *"Your laughter fills my heart with joy."* Send a verse to a favorite poem or song. Or you can write something from your heart about how you felt when you met her or how you feel being with her or what makes her special. You want to build the excitement and anticipation of a romantic evening.

Tips to remember:

- This is meant to a very romantic, sensual and tactile date. Make sure you are at that level in your relationship.
- Gifts don't have to be expensive. They are a symbol with meaning. The love notes will help build anticipation. Consider it long distance foreplay.
- Don't let her drive. Have candles all over the house. Create a Zen-like romantic ambience.
- No heavy meals. Have some flatbreads and wine by the fireplace.
- After dinner, pour some bubbly and feed strawberries to each other. It is all about romancing her senses.
- Be Tactile. Touch her hair. Gaze into her eyes. Caress her skins softly and slowly. Massage her feet. Be slow and deliberate.

This is about connecting on a very real romantic and tactile level. Don't rush anything. Even if you do make love, build up the anticipation to a night of slow and deep physical connection. Are you both literary? Then, read a poem or verse you feel represents her or how you feel. If the love you feel moves to the bedroom, make sure you have something sexy and new waiting for her. Perhaps a spa type robe, which she can use after your couples bubble bath. Or have some aromatherapy massage oils to use for giving each other a sensual massage while soft music plays in the background. Enjoy and take your time over each muscle or body part.

A few more Tips to remember::

- If this is going to move to the bedroom, make sure you have clean sheets on your bed.
- Think ahead, have towels and bubble bath and be ready to draw a bath. Remember the candles.
- Have a new soft comfortable spa-robe waiting on the bed with some massage oils and rose petals or a sexy negligeé.
- This date is not about the end result, it is about the sensual journey.

Suggestions and information:

- You can get massage oils at any health aids store or pharmacy.
- You can order from Target:
  www.target.com/c/accessories-spa-massage-health-beauty/-/N-5xtz8

- Massage oils and accessories can be gotten on-line. You can try: *www.spabodyworkmarket.com/*
- You can shop for spa-robes on Amazon or on-line at: *www.luxurysparobes.com/*

Leave the hustle and bustle of life outside the bedroom. Take a night to have one of the slowest and most sensual evenings with your loved one all the while letting her know how special she is and how much you love her. It will open hearts and you will feel bonded after such a lofty and deliberate night. If you want to add some humor to the night and act like it is Paris, you can put on French music, serve brie and crackers and baguettes, wear a beret, have champagne and perhaps, Oooh La La, speak with a French accent or in French (or whatever other country or theme you want to play out). That will add an element of fun and frivolity to the evening, if you so choose.

12 Grunge ($ to $$ / ♥ to ♥♥)

Do you like activities or places that are no frills or have a seedy or "honky tonk" feel to it? Does your gal like to throw on some lip gloss, put her hair in a ponytail and just chill with a beer? If you want a low key evening, there are plenty of affordable options.

DATE	COST	ROMANCE
Billiards	$ - $$	♥♥
Darts	$	♥
Laser Tag	$ - $$	♥♥
Beer and Pong	$	♥

Things to consider:
- If your date only wants 5-star outings, then pick another date!
- There is very little planning except for perhaps a simple internet search.
- Meant to be a *get to know you* date or a simple but romantic date. You can ramp up the date romance whenever you want.
- This is an inexpensive date with few frills.

Things you may need:
A sense of fun, good aim, like a good cold beer, love coupons or IOUs.

Tips to remember:
- Each date has a "bet" element you can have fun with in order to fuel some flirting. Figure out your bets or you can use some Love Coupons or IOUs. It just adds a little spice to the date. Print some coupons that you can download, or make your own.

Suggestions and information:
- Search the internet for sites with Love Coupons and IOUs. Here are some useful links to download some love coupons or make your own:
  > *www.rom101.com/lovecoupons.jsp*
  > *couponsformylover.com/love-coupons.aspx*
  > *www.withluv.com/printables/love-coupons.aspx*

A. Billiards

Find a cool place with attitude that has billiards and waltz your lady in. Get her set up with a beer and then hit the billiard table. Maybe you can act out scenes from two notable pool/billiards movies — *Hustler* and *Color of Money*. Or, make the billiards game more interesting and play for a prize. Play using love coupons – whoever wins gets a love coupon from the loser! Use your imagination and make it as G rated or X rated as you want! This will be a relaxing night out where you can let your hair down and just hang with people who love the precision of pool as much as you do.

B. Darts

We like darts but Mariann is terrible at darts. You just have to make sure that no one is within 180 degrees of her so she doesn't injure them. Don't want to stay in but don't want to go fancy? Instead of getting a meal at a glitzy overpriced bar with pretentious wannabe's, find a down home bar with some interesting beer options and darts and see who has the best aim to hit a bulls eye. If you are into drinking, then you can make it a drinking game. If you are into sex, then you can make it a sex game. Although, that part might need to wait until you get home! Just be careful, they say the more you drink, the worse your aim becomes. Be prepared to pay up on the bet if you lose. But, maybe being a loser is really winning. You can figure that out between the two you.

C. Laser Tag

The first time Mariann played laser tag was on her 30th birthday. She had a blast. In a controlled environment it was part aggression, part game and part exhilaration. She admits, she was easily distracted by the really cute guy on the opposite team who she wanted to kill — not literally — with a laser, of course!

This is just a thrilling and illuminating time that allows you to partner with each other and shoot the bad guy or play opposite each other and test your wills and skills as to who will win. After laser tag, find a honky tonk bar for drinks and appetizers. Or, maybe you want to play your own version of Laser Tag at home.

D. Beer and Pong

Growing up, each of our families had a ping pong table. Our respective brothers always seemed to win with their fast speed hard shots. They deflated many a ping pong ball with their powerful swap at the little plastic sphere. If you and your gal love to drink or enjoy stepping back in time to competitive ping pong challenges with your siblings, then Beer and Pong are for you. Relax in the casual atmosphere accented with the spirit of competition and the silliness of whacking a plastic ball with a paddle all while having a few drinks to just enjoy. We are not ones to judge, but if you want to use that paddle later on after you get home, well, that's up to you. But, if you're going to play a lot of ping pong, be sure to buy extra balls!

Or just play **Beer Pong**: Fill plastic cups halfway with beer. Hit the ping pong balls at the cups and if your ball lands in a cup of beer you get to drink it!

13. Heart Skipping – Don't Miss A Beat! ($ to $$$ / ♥ to ♥♥♥)

If you or your lady love can't get enough heart thumping thrills and is always looking for the next new adventure or buzz, then keep the exploration going with some great activities that will rev your engines!

DATE	COST	ROMANCE
Race Car	$ - $$$	♥♥
Bungee Jumping	$ - $$	♥
Parachuting	$ - $$	♥♥
Zip Lining	$ - $$	♥♥
Hang Gliding	$ - $$$	♥♥♥
Gun Range	$ - $$	♥
Off Road / All-Terrain Vehicles	$ - $$	♥♥

Things to consider:
- These dates are *thrill rides* and can vary from inexpensive to pricey.
- Meant for the girl who has a great spirit of adventure and can't get enough stomach dropping thrills. If she has a weak stomach or fear of heights – stay away!
- This can be a low key adventure to heart racing romantic. That level is up to you.
- These dates require some planning and reservations. Once you are there, just have fun.
- You'll bond closer as you face your fears or explor your sense of thrill seeking together!

Things you may need:
A sense of adventure, no fear, backpack, Dramamine.

A. Race Car

Ever dream of driving in a NASCAR race or a Mercedes at 100mph on the Audubon? Fast cars are sexy. Race cars are even sexier. Love the idea of putting on a helmet and squeezing into the tight compartment of a beautiful machine racing around corners and accelerating on the straightaway? You can do that! Oh yes you can! You can reserve a race car and take it for a spin around the track. Google this or visit *www.xperiencedays.com* as they have a variety of cool and interesting activities they can arrange for you.

Tips to remember:
- Make sure she likes speed and is into this kind of adventure. Otherwise, it will be an expensive failed date.
- If romance is the pursuit of adventure and thrills, then is a very romantic date. This date has sexy written all over it, so make it flirty, fun and sexy!
- Be sensitive if she backs out. No problem, you just take over the wheel!

Suggestions and information:
- Go onto Google, Yahoo or Bing to search adventures. Or, you can get on *www.xperiencedays.com* as they have a variety of cool and interesting activities they can arrange for you. This site is great too because you can also purchase gift certificates for this or for a wide range of other exciting ideas!
- Want to make this a themed gift. Well, go to your local chocolatier (candy store) and get a chocolate race car or go to a toy store and get a matchbox or toy race car. Package it and place it in a racing helmet with a sexy love note about giving her some thrills!

Go make your girlfriend's heart race a beat with love — have a blast!

B. Bungee Jumping

Some people love heights and the free-falling feeling in the pit of their stomach. If that sounds like you and your gal, then bungee jumping is for you. Mariann once agreed to the Tower Of Terror at Universal Studios in Florida and that was ten seconds of pure hell. But, her friends loved it and repeated the ride over and over. If your gal is one who loves the anticipation of a pulsating thrill and experiencing something unique or even overcoming a fear, then race to plan this date — take a scenic ride so you can count to three and jump off a cliff attached to a big rubber band!

Tips to remember:
- Make sure your date likes heights and wants to bungee jump.
- If she chickens out at the last minute and a little encouragement doesn't do the trick, then be respectful and don't force her!
- Make sure the bungee jumping company is reputable and their safety record is perfect.
- You might want to make sure your life insurance payments are current (OK, sort of joking).

If you have the funds and humor, you may want to include a gift certificate for a spa so your amour can get a neck and back massage after being tossed about like a dog toy. But, hey, if you are both up for it then go and have a thrill. Although, you may want to eat *after* the jump. Just a thought!

C. Parachuting

Mariann gets vertigo standing on the ground, so parachuting for her would be torturous. Sharon is on the same page as Mariann regarding heights. But we have friends who parachute on a regular basis. They love the heights and the initial fast descent and then the controlled fall to earth as their perspective of the sky and the earth change every second. Some do it in tandem and others are so experienced they can go it alone. But, if your girlfriend loves new experiences or this is on her bucket list, then by all means, grab this once in a lifetime experience. It will be a great story to share with friends and at parties.

Tips to remember:
- Make sure she wants to parachute.
- Discuss going and take her or surprise her. Perhaps get her a book or DVD on parachuting and gift wrap is with a note card or gift certificate.
- Be sensitive if she backs out and don't force her!
- Make sure the company is reputable and their safety record is perfect.

If she likes heights and thrills she will be smiling and hugging you afterwards! And even if it scares her, she will still be rushing into your arms for comfort, which I am sure you will welcome! Either way – you win!

D. Zip Lining

Heights and speed are the foundation of zip lining. If you both like to hike, you can combine a hike with zip lining. Sharon has been to some parks where they have zip-line courses where you can zoom from one area of the park to the next. This can be a challenging and exhilarating experience. If you don't know a place, just Google it and you'll soon discover where you can take your date for a different kind of hike in the park!

Tips to remember:
- If she seems enthused by zip lining, then plan the day.
- Do a little research to find zip lining adventures or courses near you.
- Check out the safety record of the course before you commit.

E. Hang Gliding

Do you yearn to feel like a bird and for a short while understand what it's like to fly high above the earth under your own control? If experiencing this seems exhilarating to you and your lady, then hang gliding just maybe an ideal afternoon date for you. If we were not afraid of heights, we would try this adventure.

Tips to remember:
- This is done in select areas and can be pricey to try. Be prepared. Know for sure you both want to try this adventure before you commit.
- Be sensitive, it's OK if she backs out. Do make sure the safety record and reputations of the people and companies conducting the hang gliding are accident free!

This certainly is a once in a lifetime experience that will get your adrenaline going and expand your perspective.

F. Gun Range

If you and your gal find guns morally wrong or politically incorrect, then skip this section. But, if your gal has talked about wanting to know what shooting a gun feels like or the power behind specially crafted metal feels like in her hand, then why not go to a shooting range one day? It's safe and you can both test your skills on a target.

Tips to remember:
- A simple internet search will result in a shooting range listing near you.
- Make sure your gal is not turned off by using a gun.

Suggestions and information:
- For those who really love guns and are in Vegas, there is a place to go that has all kinds of weapons (hand guns, semi-automatic and full automatic guns) where you can shoot in a safe environment. Check out *machinegunsvegas.com/about/*

G. Off Road / All-Terrain Vehicles

If your lady is a down home fun loving gal who loves the country and motorcycles or bikes, then she will enjoy riding an off road vehicle. Navigate the woody terrain, streams and landscape as you make your way in a big wheeled machine.

Tips to remember:
- You have to find some trails and an ATV rental place.
- Check out safety issues and precautions before heading out.
- Add some romance and stop at a scenic spot, spread a blanket and enjoy a few snacks and conversation.

Suggestions and information:
- Check out this organization, *www.treadlightly.org*
  They are a non-profit whose website states "their mission is to promote responsible outdoor recreation through ethics education and stewardship programs".
- Be safe and read some tips on riding off road vehicles:
  > *ezinearticles.com/?Off-Road-Vehicle-Safety---Ten-Tips-to-Increase-Safety&id=2557059*
  > *www.atvsafety.org/InfoSheets/ATV_Riding_Tips.pdf*
  > *www.artipot.com/articles/1443840/tips-for-safety-while-riding-an-off-road-vehicle.htm*

You can rent them and enjoy a free-spirited ride through the woods. This might become an activity you continue on a regular basis!

14 Just Plain Romantic Date
($ to $$$$$ / ♥♥♥ to ♥♥♥♥)

Sometimes you just want to take your lady on an adventure that is simply romantic. As always, something that is fun, original and imaginative is impressive to your lady and will be appreciated.

DATE	COST	ROMANCE
The Hunt (Ransom, Scavenger, Meetup)	$ - $$$	♥♥♥
Swim With The Dolphins	$ - $$$$$	♥♥♥♥
Movie Night – A Drive-In At Home	$ - $$	♥♥♥

Things to consider:

- These dates are for people who are in a serious relationship or who just want to step up their game.
- These dates involve planning, research and logistics. Be prepared!
- Meant to be really romantic or romantic with a bit of mystery thrown in for good measure.
- Make sure your gal has a sense of humor and can just "go with the flow" if she needs to.
- The most important thing to remember, no matter the activity — *It's all about the romance!*

Things you may need:

A plan, "map", notes, clues-riddles-questions, reservations (hotel and air possible), camera, video, large blanket, projector for your computer/iPad, wine, good takeout food, love note.

A. The Hunt

The various hunts described in this section involve a zigzag adventure you can do as a couple or with friends. Under **The Hunt** category, there are three options for the date. They involve planning and precise execution, to different degrees and detail. **Ransom** is the easiest with a fun end result. **Scavenger** has the most set up, planning and execution. **Meet Up** can vary in complexity and detail. Make it is a simple or complicated as you like.

Ransom

- Take something from your lady and hold it ransom.
- Then send her a text message that if she adheres to the following instructions, she will get her item back.
- Send her a link or directions to a destination (like a liquor store) where you have previously arranged for her to pick up a bottle of Champagne (already paid for). Once this is completed, she should confirm to you. Then send her to another destination via text or email. For example, to pick up whipped cream and strawberries. Once she confirms, you can text her that she is close to possibly getting her item back. Send her to the next destination — such as a bakery to pick up a speciality cake that you have already arranged and paid for.
- After sending her to three destinations, forward the final destination which is where you will be— your place, a restaurant, a hotel, a beach or a park. That final destination is up to you. Use your imagination or any combination of the date ideas in this book.

Tips to remember:

- Pick places that are not too far between each other.
- Try to pick places that are on the way to the *final* destination where you will be.
- Make sure your gal has the sense of humor and fun to appreciate this and not be the type to find it annoying or not fun.
- Make sure whatever you have her pick up is free or you have pre-arranged and paid for.
- Don't over complicate it. Make the items fun and easy to get. It's more about the mystery and the journey than what you are actually having her pick up. But, by all means, keep a theme and make the items fun. Champagne, whipped cream and chocolate covered strawberries — who wouldn't mind picking up those items?

Scavenger Hunt

- This involves several steps of planning, they include:
- Prepare a map that takes you on a journey. Take a worn piece of heavy paper and draw a map or get an image from the internet and print it on a heavy piece of paper which you can tear and crumple.

- Pre-set the map at a location where you can deliberately "stumble" across it while on a bike ride or hike that you are taking with your girlfriend. Find a way for her to find it.
- Follow the instructions on the map. Have different landmarks noted on the map. When you get to the destination, have a clue or riddle ready and set or planted that leads you to the next destination. Each destination can host a gift of meaning or a card that has one word on it or a sentiment on it (your feelings). Or it might require her to do something (e.g. kiss you on the cheek), or tell you the one thing she loves most about you, or the ability for her to ask *you* any question she wants.
- Continue following clues to local destinations in your area whether it is a suburb, beach town or metropolitan city. At the end of the journey you can have a full sentence that tells how you feel, reveals a gift or even tells her that you love her. Have some fun with this, it's a great opportunity to deliver a special message for your girl at the end of your scavenger hunt.

Tips to remember:
- You can certainly make sure she knows this is a game planned by you once you "find" the map.
- Make sure she is the type of girl to enjoy this kind of scavenger adventure.
- Use your imagination and have fun with the clues, riddles and things to do or find along the way.

Meet Up

There are steps and planning involved in the "Meet Up" version of the Scavenger Hunt date:
- Arrange to meet your date somewhere. But instead, at the time you planned to meet, text her a list of instructions she has to follow to get to you. You may also pre-set the list or have it at a store such as a bakery. Just make sure you've let the store owner or staff know that she'll be picking something up there. Just let her know via text or email. The list will outline the instructions, time limit and what she will receive upon completion.

- Give her a list of things she has to find (at a mall close by or in a park) in the next 30 minutes to an hour. Those items can range from a photo to a twig or leaves to jelly beans – whatever you want without being difficult. She then has to meet you at a destination with the things she collected. In addition to collecting things, you can also have her take photos or answer/solve riddles to get an item. When she reaches the destination, the number of items she has directly correlates to your gift from a cup of coffee to a kiss to a dinner to a massage to a cruise- well, you get the idea.
- Up front in your instructions, you can advise what she'd get depending on the number of items she gets on the list. For example, if your list has 50 things on it, then outline that if they gather fewer than 5 items on the list — they get a lemon. 10 items, a donut. 15 items — a dinner. 20 items — a massage. 50 items — a cruise. Obviously, the more items on the list she gets, the better the gift! You can be as sexy, romantic, naughty or just nice in the choice of what she gets. That's up to you.
- You can also be lurking in the shadows and follower her on the hunt and video-tape her. Later, edit the video with some music and narration for a mini-documentary memento of her experience.
- Keep time under 2 hours. An hour is preferred.

Tips to remember:
- Don't make the tasks to do or items to get too complicated or too difficult. This is all about framing a gift or doing something fun in a different way. Don't make it stressful.
- Keep the time needed to under an hour. Make getting the number of items doable within that time frame. It's a game after all.
- Make sure she enjoys this kind of scavenger adventure.
- Use your imagination and have fun with the clues and the gifts.

Please remember that in any version of the scavenger hunt game, whatever note you leave can be a riddle or question about your relationship — or anything you want. You determine how easy or complex this will be. As you can see with this date, it takes planning and preparation and some originality. You should give yourself a little time to plan it out. You don't have to go far and can always conduct a scavenger hunt indoors, your home or just on your property.

Suggestions and information:

- For the best desserts in the world, try Carlo's Bakery (aka: The Cake Boss). They have locations in Hoboken, Westfield and Ridgewood, NJ. If you want a great dessert, artisitically crafted special themed cake or sweet treats, then you must go to Carlo's Bakery - and they ship. To bring class and art to the dessert portion of your date, go to Carlo's Bakery. Their website is *www.carlosbakery.com*
- If you are in New York City, there is a scavenger hunt called, Accomplice, (*www.accomplicetheshow.com*) that is advertised as "part game, part theater, part tour" that sends you on a mission around the city. It is done with a group of people though, if that matters.
- Here is an article on "how to propose using a scavenger hunt" *www.wikihow.com/Propose-to-Her-Using-a-Scavenger-Hunt-Game*
- Need some help in planning a scavenger hunt or coming up with ideas? Here are a few links to check out
  > *www.mymysteryparty.com/scavengerhunts.html*
  > *www.wikihow.com/Play-a-Scavenger-Hunt-Game-at-a-Party*
  > *www.buzzle.com/articles/scavenger-hunt-ideas-for-adults.html*
  > *games.thefuntimesguide.com/2011/09/scavenger-hunts.php*
  > *www.ehow.com/how_7764118_set-up-scavenger-hunt-wife.html*
  > *www.scavenger-hunt-guru.com/romantic-scavenger-hunt.html*

B. Swim With The Dolphins

If your lady has always wanted to swim with the dolphins then you'll make her day with this uniquely memorable opportunity to cuddle next to these gentle mammals. Are you near a park or area that offers this? If you are then plan the day and make sure to pack a bag of snacks and change of clothing. And don't forget your camera or video! If you don't live close to such a facility, you may have to plan a special trip to achieve this wondrous event. Use hotel or airline reward points if you have them.

Tips to remember:

- Make sure this is on your girlfriend's bucket list.
- Surprise her and then plan the trip together or just take her as a surprise – you know what your gal likes or where you are in the relationship.
- Make sure you document the experience with photos and video!

If this is something you think your girl would love, try to make it happen even if you have to save your pennies over time. She will appreciate the forethought and your commitment to planning something different and amazing. Watching her swim and play with the dolphins will bring big smiles to both of your faces!

C. Movie Night — A Drive In At Home

One night, stay in and just be with your girl in a relaxed and familiar atmosphere. Order in or her favorite take-out food or cook a favorite meal. Pour a glass of wine and watch a movie. Wanna do a different take on a movie? Create your own drive-in. Set up a blanket in your backyard, get your laptop and aim a projector at the side of your house to view the film. Make some popcorn, grab a soda and your favorite box of candy and sit back and relax. Pretend you're in a drive-in and have an old fashioned high school make out session.

Tips to remember:
- This is a low key date that is just meant to be comfortable. The romance is in the simplicity of just being together, relaxing and watching a movie.
- Make sure that you get a movie she loves and you have the equipment to project onto the house.
- Make sure you have everything ready from a blanket to popcorn to candy to any beverage she likes.
- Be really sweet and use the time to hold her close.

If you want to make it extra personal, find photos and/or movies of her childhood or shots you took together. Get them produced into your own *home movie*. It will be a walk down memory lane for her and you both can relive the many wonderful times you've shared. If you'd like to surprise her with a personal and customized video, you can certainly do it yourself on your computer with simple editing software. If you don't have the equipment or the time, take the pictures and videos you want coordinated to a video services company. That could be a camera shop or photo developing store (*www.motophoto.com*) or a local video services company. I have a local video services company, Interim Business Solutions in New Jersey (*www.rgibs.com*), who produce Industrial and how-to instructional videos for companies, do promotional videos for a regional theater and create personal videos for family functions and special occasions.

Suggestions and information:
- Check out: *www.rgibs.com* and *www.motophoto.com*
- Do a Google search for companies in your area.

15 Kidnap Date ($$$$$ / ♥♥♥♥♥)

If you're gal is open to surprises (not everyone is, so find out first!) then *kidnap* her and take her on an oh-so-romantic date. This can be anything from a picnic at the local park (if you're on a tight budget) to dinner and dancing at the classiest restaurant in town or (if money is no object), a weekend away in the tropics or at a cozy cabin in the mountains. You can turn just about any date idea into a Kidnap Date. There is something naughty, edgy, dangerous and fun about this date. Make your date as simple or as elaborate as you want depending on her time and your available funds. The key point to remember is that every part of the date should be a mystery or surprise so you can keep her senses as heightened as possible at all times.

DATE	COST	ROMANCE
What Happens In Vegas Stays In Vegas	$$$$$	♥♥♥♥♥
Finally!	$$$$$	♥♥♥♥♥
B & B – Seasons Of Love	$$$$$	♥♥♥♥♥

Things to consider:
• Make sure your date is open to surprises.
• Whether it's a budget date or pricey, make this ultra-romantic.
• This is a date for when you're officially "in a relationship" and want to really impress!
• Keep up the mystery and heightened sense of suspense.
• If it's a weekend away date, you may need to enlist the aid of one of her friends or a family member to help make sure she's properly packed for the trip
• Think about how to get her packed for the trip and plan accordingly.

Things you will need:
Note cards, flowers, mode of kidnapping, transportation, arrangements for activities while at your destination, accessories for your kidnapping (fluffy fur lined hand cuffs, negligee, bag of sexy goodies), gift (if you want to), hotel and/or air reservations, a way to get her packed for a trip.

Things you will need to plan for:

- Will she need her passport? If yes, figure out how to get it.
- How can you get to pack her bags or get her to? Maybe you can enlist her friend. Or you tell her there is something up and to pack, but she does not know the details. You can build more suspense that way too.
- Does she need to take vacation time? If yes, tell her something is up so she can get the time from work.

Planning her kidnapping (aka: pickup) – Consider the following:

- If you pick her up at work, have a limo waiting – with you in it.
- Or, do you know an actor who can dress as a Police Office and as she approaches her car, he "fake arrests" her and walks her to your car or a waiting limo with you in it. Meanwhile, your actor friend can take her car and keep it safe til she returns.
- If you pick her up at home, arrive in your car or a limo. Go to the door and hand her a card. Smile. Say nothing. The card should tell her to follow you. Inside the limo have champagne and only give out tidbits of information, if at all.
- Or, knock on her door. When she answers, *kidnap* her, restrain her with fluffy pink handcuffs and haul her away!
- Perhaps you become a character (A pirate? Her favorite super-hero?) and act out a funny or romantic scene before you whisk her away.
- Try being a "Mystery Man" and put on a mask. Go to her door, hand her a note and a rose. During the drive, when you want to suggest where to go or what you have planned, do so with a note and a rose. In the car, you can speak or still play Mystery Man. Anticipate the questions she might ask and instead of speaking, hand her a note with pre-written funny, informative or sexy messages!

The key to this date is to keep it *suspenseful*. This should be a very sensory experience so each of her senses should be heightened by the mystery. Impart as little or as much information as you want. If you have a theme to your kidnapping, then by all means keep that "role playing" constant. They key here is to have fun. Remember, each hotel has a concierge who is there to help you with suggestions and arrangements. Contact them before you arrive and get their help with the arrangements for dinners, shows or excursions. Just recognize them with a tip when you do see them.

A. What Happens In Vegas Stays In Vegas

Everyone loves Vegas! Even if you are not a big gambler, there are tons of things to do in Las Vegas. Lie by the pool, spa day, shows, restaurants, people-watching, concerts, Hoover Dam, rides and games, dance clubs, comedy, dune buggy rides, driving exotic cars and helicopter rides. That's just to name a few.

Tips to remember:

- Make this trip pure fun, pure mystery and pure romance. Anticipate everything. Have a bottle of bubbly in the room waiting (or her favorite beverage).
- Give your gal the opportunity to have some approval over shows or restaurants. Keep some elements for her input.
- Don't attend a show every night. Make sure your schedule has flexibility and is not too structured.
- Definitely make time to see the sites of Vegas such as the gondola ride at the Venetian, the light show at the Bellagio, the aquarium at Mandalay Bay, the original Vegas strip, and the Wax Museum. We hate buffets, but the buffet at the Encore is great!
- Set aside time to languish by the pool or have a couples massage. Or, go back to your room for a lazy afternoon of lovemaking.
- When the time is right, give her a cute little sexy gift bag with some things naughty and some things nice. If you forget, there are some great shops in Vegas to shop together for some sexy items.

Suggestions and information:

- Here is a good site for attractions and things to do in Vegas: *www.vegas.com/attractions/*
- An article on the top 100 things to do in Vegas: *govegas.about.com/od/attractions/a/100thingstodo.htm*
- Trip Advisor has great reviews and travel information. Definitely worthwhile to check them out: *www.tripadvisor.com/Attractions-g45963-Activities-Las_Vegas_Nevada.html*

Vegas has phenomenal restaurants so go and delight your palate! Don't be so regimented in your plans and allow for spontaneity. We somehow suspect you will get lucky in Vegas.

B. Finally!

Is there one thing that your girlfriend has always wanted to do? Is it a play she's dying to see or her favorite band that never seems to tour? Take matters into your own hands and plan to make that wish a reality. Just go on-line and buy the tickets. If out of town, then make it an overnight adventure. Enlist her friend to get her to believe they are going away for a night so she has her clothes and toiletries packed. Again, kidnap her and make sure she has no details. So when you walk into the concert hall she will squeal with excitement. If it is that elusive play, then beware as she may not stop smiling. Plan a great dinner that is in line with what she likes whether that's BBQ, cozy Italian, steakhouse or romantic French bistro. You may have to travel out of town for both. Remain silent and build the mystery and make sure she is dressed appropriately or take with you the items she needs.

Tips to remember:
- Listen to your girlfriend and really find that one thing she keeps talking about but never gets to do. Then you have your idea.
- Plan everything around that, be it day excursion or an overnight trip.

Suggestions and information:
- Here are good sites for plays and concerts if that falls into the scope of your planning:
  > *www.ticketmaster.com*
  > *www.telecharge.com*
  > *www.playbill.com*

Mariann was dating someone a few years ago who loved a small and locally known but somewhat obscure band that did not tour much. Well, she checked their site and they were playing locally, so she planned a surprise night out. Her boyfriend was not into surprises, but she kept the mystery alive. He loved the pub atmosphere for dinner and was surprised the band was playing so near. He told her later that night, *"but people don't do this kind of stuff for me."* She said, *"well, I guess you are hanging out with the wrong people."* This experience will tell your girlfriend she is hanging out with the right person!

C. B & B — Seasons Of Love

If going somewhere that can be reached by car is preferred, then plan a lazy weekend where you can lounge in each other's arms and be spontaneous if the desire hits you. Pick her favorite time of year whether it is the flowers blossoming in spring or the leaves changing in fall. Plan a long weekend at a really pretty quaint and comfortable bed & breakfast. Maybe you go to the Berkshires in Massachusetts and enjoy the spectacular views of October's changing leaves. Or go when the music festival is running. Or, head to the Finger Lakes, NY region and stay at one of the wineries connected with a hotel. A quick on-line search will find bed & breakfasts at scenic areas near you.

Tips to remember:

- Put some planning into this even to make it casual. Plan a picnic lakeside, rent a bike and enjoy the countryside, hire a private boat on a lake, river or ocean. Find an arty town and stroll along main street hand in hand.
- Keep the mystery alive by making this romantic and celebrating being a couple all the while making her feel special.
- Plan a special private dinner where you only have eyes for each other.
- Incorporate elements such as a love note, gift, love coupons, massage oils, bubble bath, champagne, sexy novel, negligee, flowers or scented candle.
- Remember, it's not the cost of anything you give, it's the gesture and thoughtfulness behind it that underscores *you get her and understand her.*

Suggestions and information:

- Here are some great sites that provide a listing of Bed and Breakfasts in the USA by state:
  > *www.bedandbreakfast.com/usa.html*
  > *www.resortsandlodges.com/bed-and-breakfasts/usa/index.html*
  > *www.bbon-line.com/united-states/*

You will have a great time and she will be surprised, relaxed and happy!

16 Marriage Proposal Date
($ to $$$ / ♥♥♥ to ♥♥♥♥♥)

Congratulations! You've met someone, fallen in love and have now made the biggest decision of your life — to ask that special lady to marry you. That's great! You are so lucky to have found your soul mate. The kind of marriage proposal you plan will be part you and part what you think will make her say *Yes* before you even finish asking. Is your soon to be fiancé low key and casual? Is she nerdy and intellectual? A free spirit who loves adventure? An erotic soul who loves a smoldering evening? A sports fan? Or someone who wants to feel like Cinderella or loves top shelf five-star service and sophistication all the way? Only you can answer that question. Note that many of the dates in this book can be adapted to suit a marriage proposal date. You'll just need to tweak them a bit to customize them for your soon-to-be fiancé.

DATE	COST	ROMANCE
Sunrise	$ - $$	♥♥♥♥♥
Antiquing – Follow The Road Show	$ - $$$	♥♥♥♥
Football, Baseball and Basketball – Oh My!	$ - $$$	♥♥♥
Smokin' Hot Jazz	$$-$$$	♥♥♥♥♥
Just Plain Romantic- Scavenger Hunt - A Different Twist	$ - $$$	♥♥♥

Things to consider:
- This is a very special date and one of the most important experiences of your life.
- You can plan a dinner or hike or secret get-away as well so follow one of the dates in any section and tweak it for a marriage proposal.
- The romance needs to be off the charts. Pull out the stops and make every moment of this experience memorable.
- This date requires planning and logistics and adding elements that are outside the box.
- Don't forget the ring!

Things you may need:

Big comfy blanket, picnic basket, champagne, food, real plates and glasses and cutlery, rose or flowers, love note, make a memory book, rose petals, sexy gift bag, engagement ring.

A. Sunrise

There is something magical about a sunrise as the dawning of a new day makes everything seem possible. The sun peers and smiles from just beyond the horizon and in a short time, it is perched with a wide grin greeting your day with happiness and hopefulness. If your gal is a morning person, suggest a lazy and relaxing morning watching the sunrise.

Tips to remember:

- This date requires coordination and is romantic yet casual.
- Put careful planning into what you want to serve for your picnic on the beach at sunrise. Prepare a nice breakfast with croissants and butter, Danish, coffee (thermos) and anything else you feel would be appetizing. If you can arrange it, have real plates and glasses and silverware versus plastic. And if she is into the bubbly, have mimosas ready to celebrate.
- Really make sure to set the atmosphere. Make it cozy. Pull her close to you and really feel a sense of tranquil togetherness. Wrap a blanket around you both and snuggle. Speak softly into her ear about how much she means to you.
- Underscore the morning with some music on your iPod/speakers. Plan especially what you want played so that it contributes to the mood you want to create.
- When to propose is up to you. Perhaps when the sun is on the horizon or has perched itself in the sky. Or, during breakfast just before the sky becomes bright with sun. Maybe you tell her that you want to celebrate being with her, pull out the bubbly and drop the ring into the champagne flute (glass please!) or your toast is the marriage proposal. You have to feel the situation and be open to when the right time is.

After she says *yes*, then just lie in each other's arms full of gratitude as you watch and hear the soft sounds of the ocean waves against the shore.

B. Antiquing — Follow the Road Show

Does your girl like rides on country roads? Covered wooden bridges? Gazebos? Throwing pebbles into a stream? Stopping into quaint antique shops to find interesting treasures? Sitting on a swing by a lake or the relaxing movement of a rocking chair on an old Victorian porch? How about a canopied bed with oil-lit lamps by the bedside and lace curtains? Well, a perfect proposal could take place while dining privately in the gazebo of a quaint B & B in a green tree or autumn tree-filled background overlooking a small serene lake.

Tips to remember:

- This date will take planning especially as it relates to the dinner, if that's when you plan to propose.
- Work with the inn owners to make arrangements. Have them set up a table on a private piece of the property, or by a lake or in a Gazebo. Plan a special meal that favors what she likes.
- If you really want to add some extra romance, hire a harpist or violinist to play in the background and serenade her.
- Keep the weekend relaxed and fun so that she does not expect it.
- Have an idea of things to do in the area before you get there.
- How to propose is up to you. Perhaps when they bring dessert in a silver covered dish. Take her hand to propose with the ring in the covered dish. Or, simply get down on bended knee and propose. Or put a rose on her plate with the ring around the stem. You know what she likes, so think about how she would like to be proposed to.
- If you want to propose with sweets, order a specialty themed cake that is ornately decorated and asks "Will You Marry Me?" Carlo's Bakery (of Cake Boss fame) makes the most delicious desserts that are works of art. If you are in the NY/NJ area, you can pick it up. If you can't, they ship! Who can say NO to cake and a proposal? Make sure to check out Carlo's Bakery at *www.carlosbakery.com*

The important thing is that you have met and fallen in love with someone and are illustrating how much you love and appreciate her by being thoughtful, creative and caring in how you propose. We know she will say yes. With the love, thoughtfulness and effort that you exhibited with this proposal, she may say yes before you finish asking!

More Tips to remember:

- If you really want to be all sweet and mushy, make a *Memory Book*. This can be a book of photos or verses or experiences or things about her that you love. It's a celebration of her and of you as a couple.
- If you do decide to give her the memory book, consider your proposal being the last page of the book. As your lady looks through the book, you can perhaps have a message asking her to marry you or a pic of the ring. It will take her a moment to figure it out and then you propose. Use your imagination and ideas will flood into your mind!

While you are dining, make sure the Inn Keepers have tidied your room, placed some candles around and have a bottle of bubbly waiting. Spread some rose petals on the bed, she'll love it. You might also have a pretty negligee waiting under her pillow — as a sexy surprise. Congratulations! Now go and *celebrate* the next chapter of your life together.

C. Football, Baseball and Basketball — Oh My!

We admit it, we are not professional sports fans. Will we go to a game? *Sure*. Will we buy season tickets? *No*. We have friends who are die-hard football, hockey, basketball and baseball fans. If the that girl in your life is crazy for sports and you want to make her your wife, then you might consider a rousing night out at a sporting event. If you have the funds, maybe you tell your gal that you scored great tickets to see your favorite team and you want to celebrate by taking a limo to the event. Decide to make it a sensational night out on the town.

Tips to remember:

- This date will take coordination depending on how you propose. If you plan to pop the question in the stands or at a sports bar afterward, then there's very little planning.
- If you are confident and want to go *big*, perhaps you get brought down to the field during half time and propose in front of 20,000 people.
- Or, you arrange to have the question posted on the Jumbotron.
- If you want to get on the field or use the Jumbotron, I recommend you call the team office, tell them your plans and make a plea to help you. There may be a charge. If not, and they agree to do this for you, be

nice and appreciative. Make sure to send them a thank you note and a gift basket to the person who helped you.
- If you really want to step up the luxury, hire a limo. On the way to the game, give her a jersey of her favorite player. On the way home or to eat, have flowers and champagne waiting to celebrate.
- If you want to ratchet up the night even more, plan a surprise night at a hotel (just make sure you have her clothes and toiletries pre-packed).

Building a date or proposal around the framework of what your lady likes shows that you understand her. When a woman feels understood she feels loved and appreciated. That is an aphrodisiac to many women.

Suggestions and information:
- The following sites are good sources to send flowers, a fruit arrangement or gift basket:
  > *www.ftd.com (Flowers)*
  > *www.ediblearrangements.com (fruit arrangements)*
  > *www.gourmetgiftbaskets.com*

D. Smokin' Hot Jazz

Some women ooze a smokey sensuality. They like the fine smooth side of life that involves good food, good wine and good jazz. Break out your inner Barry White and pour on the smooth charm and sexuality. This type of evening will leave her cooing by the end of the night. Plan a hot night out at a jazz and dinner show.

Tips to remember:
- You decide when to propose — over dinner or after her favorite song. Or, you can arrange with the band to have you go to the stage while the band underscores your proposal with some smooth music. The venue should help arrange this for you. Again, recognize any assistance with a card, money or gift basket to those who helped you.
- Do you sing or play a musical instrument? Maybe you can get to go on stage and jam a bit. When you are done, go to the mic and propose. If you sing, you can perform a romantic ballad and finish it off with either a proposal from stage, or privately when you're back at your table.

Plans afterward are up to you. They can include going back to your place or a hotel or continuing the night at an after-hours bar, cigar bar, rooftop bar or your favorite dessert place — a place you know your fiancé will love.

However you plan the logistics of the evening, you will start and end your smoky hot night with fire and long burning embers. Wow, after that we need a tall glass of cold water!

E. Just Plain Romantic — Scavenger Hunt — A Different Twist

There is a date in our **Just Plain Romantic** section called, **The Scavenger Hunt**. You can do the scavenger hunt, but with a twist at the end.

Scavenger Hunt

- This involves several steps of planning:
- Prepare a map that takes you on a journey. Take a worn piece of heavy paper and draw a map or get an image from the internet and print it on a heavy piece of paper which you can tear and crumple.
- Pre-set the map at a location where you deliberately "stumble" across the map while on a bike ride or hike that you and your girlfriend have planned. Find a way for her to find it.
- Follow the instructions on the map. Have different landmarks noted on the map. When you get to the destination, have a clue or riddle already set that leads you to the next destination. Each destination can host a gift of meaning or a card with one word or sentiment on it (your feelings). It might require her to do something (e.g. kiss you on the cheek, or tell you the one thing she loves most about you, the ability for her to ask you any question she wants).
- Continue to local destinations whether it is a suburb, beach town or metropolitan city. *At journey's end you can ask her to marry you*. Your gift at the final destination might be a box of cracker jacks where you have hidden a fake ring. When she finds the ring you propose, reveal the real diamond and pop the question. This will be very unexpected!
- Not ready to purchase all of those little gifts? Here's something simpler: collect alphabetical letters or phrases along that way that spell out WILL YOU MARRY ME?

17 The Married Couple Date
($ to $$$ / ♥♥♥ to ♥♥♥♥)

Just because you are married doesn't mean you can't keep the romance alive nor does it mean you can't date your spouse. Kids, jobs, parents, and household chores all seem to take priority with most couples. Yes, things need to be accomplished, but you can't ignore the person you are traveling this very important life journey with. If you forget about yourselves as a couple, you will stop being a couple. You will become ships passing in the night and you won't be able to see each through the hazy fog of life. *Do Not Let This Happen!* The only way this won't is if you put energy into your relationship with your spouse. And this isn't some form of water torture, this is fun. It is OK and necessary to have a spirited life. It's a great way to stay younger too!

DATE	COST	ROMANCE
Cooking For Two	$ - $$	♥♥♥
Painting Lessons In The Park	$ - $$$	♥♥♥
Moonlight	$ - $$	♥♥♥♥

Things to consider:
• These dates focus on re-connecting and making sure you express romance and thoughtfulness.
• Some of the dates require more planning, logistics or research than others.
• Romance for these dates can be subtle and loving to off the charts. That is up to you!
• Focus on getting back to what you both loved about each other and re-ignite your passion.

Things you may need:

Research cooking schools or restaurants with lessons, art/painting lessons with a school or artist, art supplies, big comfy blanket, picnic basket, champagne or wine, food, rose or flowers, love note or card, journal, pens, iPod/speakers.

Sharon's parents, through most of their marriage, had date night every Saturday. They discovered new restaurants doing this and made sure they had alone time at least once a week, away from kids, chores and home distractions. We think that's why they had a great and loving marriage!

A. Cooking For Two

The Food Network really propelled cooking to the forefront of new things to do as an individual or as a couple. Restaurants are opening up with all kinds of interesting fusion oriented menus. Cuisine is becoming more varied and people are more daring in sampling tasty delights. Cooking is gratifying. You not only have something to show for it, but you get to eat it. Why not suggest taking cooking lessons with your spouse? Perhaps one night at dinner or while you are having a cup of tea and a snack before bed, hand your wife a wrapped cooking book with an invitation to take a lesson. You can have the date planned or agree on a day to book the next morning. Make the day as romantic as you want.

Tips to remember:

• Make this date about bonding over a new or existing interest that you love doing together.
• If you just want the experience, go for a one day or one session class. If you are both more serious about expanding your expertise in the kitchen, then go for something held once a week for several weeks. Depends on your available time and funds.
• Many times in these cooking classes, you eat what you have just learned to cook. Add some romance and give her flowers before you eat and take her favorite wine for the dinner.
• If you want to keep the evening going, then go to your favorite dessert place or find a funky and cozy music venue to end the evening with some tunes and drinks.

Suggestions and information:

• If you are in New York City, try ICE (Institute of Culinary Education), *www.iceculinary.com/*. Google Culinary School or Cooking School or Cooking Lessons in your city.
• Check your local papers for listings of restaurants that might offer

a cooking lesson. Or check the adult education listings. We think a restaurant or cooking school is far more romantic but is probably more costly. There are even kitchenware stores that offer cooking lessons.

- If you want to try something really serious and abroad, then try the Cordon Blue Cooking school in Paris or London.

Your palate will surely appreciate it and so will your wife!! So, go to it — "Allez Cuisiner!"

B. Painting Lesson In The Park

Life is busy. With jobs and personal responsibilities, it's easy to lose yourself in day-to-day routines. The key here is to stop and reflect on your passions and why you love your wife and reconnect with her. Perhaps your wife has an artistic flare or the soul of a writer or painter. When we align with people or activities that we are passionate about, life becomes fuller and more meaningful. You eliminate any sense that you gave up everything because of work and/or family. Is your wife a Van Gogh in hiding? Did she paint once long ago and misses it? Well, give her the gift of reconnecting with her passion and creative self. Your confidence and support of your wife in what she loves to do will mean more than words can express. One idea is to surprise her by setting up a painting lesson for her with an artist or art teacher.

Tips to remember:
- Plan something out of the ordinary. Find an artist who will give a lesson in the park.
- You can tell her what is going on, or surprise her. Depends on if she likes surprises.
- Celebrate her creativity or interest. Be supportive.
- Is she out of art supplies? Visit an art supply store and get her what she needs and have it ready for her when you go.

The same can be done with other passions such as writing. Go to a writing conference or a day long seminar. Arrange a one or two hour private session with a known writer/teacher to review your wife's work. The instructor will go through her work with her. You can contact the dean or a teacher at a writing school or contact the administrators of a writing conference for a recommendation. Regardless of the passion, you can find a way to reconnect your wife back to something that resonates with her soul.

Suggestions and information:
- Go to a nearby art store to pick up what you need. Not sure? Ask!
- Go to a bookstore and pick up a pretty journal, pen, books on writing or writing supplies to fuel your wife's artistic imagination. It's a great show of support!
- Google what you are looking for. We Googled painting lessons in central park and up came a link to an artist who *taught lessons in the park*. It was the perfect background to find an inspirational subject.

Mariann did this for someone once. He loved it. The art lesson was in the park and she took the lesson too. The teacher looked at Mariann's non-work of art, scrunched his face and said, *"well, it's not terrible."* Her date was obviously the one with talent. By acknowledging your wife's interests, she will appreciate your caring efforts and help to renew something that is important to her. Showing your understanding will not only revitalize your wife, but will rejuvenate your relationship. Just don't tell her that her painting is *"not that terrible."*

C. Moonlighting

Sharon is a sucker for an ocean and moonlit nights. Or, on a hill overlooking a pretty valley. That time between sunset and moonrise, to her, is magical! So, plan a picnic at sunset.

Tips to remember:
- Keep it simple, low key and peaceful.
- Ensure you have a soft cushy blanket to put on the sand and another to snuggle under.
- Open your favorite wine and have some snacks available in case she is hungry. Nothing fancy — some cookies or cheese and crackers (don't forget the cheese knife) or some finger pastries or truffles if she has a sweet tooth. This date is *not* about the food.
- Bring a journal and pens and write down how you feel about each other or why you love each other. Keep the journals and write notes back

and forth to each other even after the picnic and the sun has set. Make it something you do whenever you have your date night. Be silly or romantic — whatever fits the mood.

- Perhaps you don't want to keep a journal going, so just write a card to each other and then read it aloud. The openness of heart, mind and spirit will bring you closer.
- It's nighttime, so think ahead and make sure you have bug spray, water, tissues or anything practical that will help make the experience run smoothly.

Maybe stay the night under the stars where you may both be moved to make love — that's up to you. Either way, a tranquil night staring at the moon and the stars with the person you love most snuggled beside you is a pretty awesome night. Have fun!

18 Outdoorsy Date ($ to $$$ / ♥ to ♥♥)

Everyone these days seems to have a focus on health and healthy living, which is great. Some people are avid adventurers and explorers and really relate with nature and the outdoors. Mariann skied once and wound up in the ER, had an operation and was in a leg brace for nine months — all on her way *to* the skiing lesson. So, for Mariann, skiing is out. But, she does do drinks by the fireplace very, very well. There are a plethora of activities and ideas you can do outdoors. Below are just a handful, but we think you'll get the idea.

DATE	COST	ROMANCE
Paintball	$ - $$	♥
Biking	$ - $$	♥
Relive The Olympics	$ - $$$	♥♥
Hiking	$ - $$	♥♥
Rock Climbing – Indoors	$ - $$	♥
Gym / Yoga	$ - $$	♥
Fruit Farms	$ - $$	♥♥
Tennis	$ - $$	♥
Skiing / Snowmobiling / Tubing	$ - $$	♥♥
Ice Skating	$ - $$	♥

Things to consider:

• These dates are an economical and casual way to get to know your date.
• If it is early in the dating process, then the romance level may be minimal. If you are in a more serious or committed relationship, then you can increase the romance.
• You can increase the romance level with a picnic, drinks by a fire in a lodge, cocoa at a café overlooking the ice rink or relaxing over a nice, healthy dinner.
• These dates are low key. Keep in mind, women are conscious of what they are wearing and how they look and smell. So, if you are going to do anything afterward, give your gal the chance or venue to change and clean up somewhere.

- These dates don't require much planning. Just do an internet search.
- Use these dates to bond over a common interest or have a really good conversation!

Things you may need:

Gym bag with items, supplies for outdoor hike, etc. (e.g. bug spray, water), change of clothes, picnic items/basket.

A. Paintball

OK, we have to admit this appeals to our inner tom boy. As the youngest cousin, Mariann grew up around all boys. Her girl cousins were all ten years or more older than her. Of course she was going to join in and play cowboys and indians with her boy cousins. Whereas we love all things girly, there is still that 8 year old inside of Mariann who loves to play with the boys and do traditionally non-girly type activities.

Tips to remember:
- On this date, you will both work up a sweat. Make sure your girl is open to this and running around for a few hours.
- I understand the shots can hurt. So, bring extra padding. But be careful. If she finds it is not for her or is fearful, then stop or don't go!
- It's a great way to show your protective side – you don't want someone shooting your girl!
- You can go as a couple or make it a group date with your friends.

If you Google *paintball* you can find locations near you. Mariann jokes that when she tries paintball, she is going to wear an armor of bubble wrap under the protective clothing. She only hopes she doesn't get too distracted *popping* the bubble wrap and gets "shot." That would be bad. So, if your gal has an inner tomboy and is not opposed to using a paint gun, then go paint the town red - or yellow - or blue – well, you get the idea!

B. Biking

Biking can be vigorous or carefree. It is healthy and safe and you can be master over where you go or how far you bike or for how long. Rent a bike or bring your own to the beach and bike along the pathway. Go to a national state park or find an area with bike trails and cycle around watching the pretty landscape! Be safe. Be sure your tires and bike are in good condition and that you have water. Don't forget to wear a helmet. It may not be fashion forward, but it will keep you safe.

Tips to remember:
- Know the capability and experience level of your girlfriend. You don't want to do all uphill if she hasn't been on a bike in many years.
- Look into bike routes or locations before you go. If you are renting, just make sure you know where the rental place is and bring your license and money!
- Be sure to take water along for the ride.
- If you're interested in spending more time with her, pack snacks and scope out a pretty place to stop and be alone or go for a bite afterwards.

C. Relive The Olympics

Are you or your lady love fanatics of the Olympics and glued to the TV when they are on? Do you really enjoy all the sports they play? Well, why don't you pick which season you like —winter or summer sports — then determine which activities you like or want to do and set yourself on the road to a destination where the Olympics were held. For example, are you a fan of skiing? Well, take a trip to one of the sites. Tour the area and find memorabilia from the games. Take advantage of any activities that are open, especially those reflective of the Olympics! You can make these adventures international too.

Tips to remember:
- This can be a day trip or overnight trip depending on where you are in your relationship and to the closest Olympic Village.
- Many locations that have hosted the Olympics offer tours and use of the facilities!

Suggestions and information:
- The Olympics were held in: Salt Lake City, UT – Atlanta, GA – Lake Placid, NY – Squaw Valley, CA – St. Louis, MO

- For information on the sites, check out:
  www.olympic.org/united-states-of-america
- For international Olympic locations, check out:
  en.wikipedia.org/wiki/List_of_Olympic_Games_host_cities

D. Hike

Hikes are a great setting to relax and experience nature while enjoying a casual date. Hikes allow you time to find out more about each other. They can vary from pretty, scenic hikes, to more athletic hikes over mountainous terrain. If you are both experienced hikers, it can be your activity together where you can talk, hold hands and just enjoy your surroundings.

Tips to remember:
- This can be a lazy afternoon exploring or a rigorous workout. That depends on the experience and athletic level of you and your lady.
- Remember water. If it will be a long hike, bring snacks (e.g. protein bars). If more casual and explorative, then perhaps a picnic lunch.
- If you go out for a bite after and a change of clothes is necessary, let your date know so she can plan accordingly.
- Research hiking trails before you go and know where you are going. Make sure the difficulty level of the trails fits your experience level.

One time, Mariann went hiking in the mountains of North Carolina with someone who was quite experienced. The hike was challenging but they reached the top of the mountain, climbed atop some rocks and lunched looking out over the vast rich green valleys and artistically carved mountains. It was a day and a sight she will never forget.

E. Rock Climbing — Indoors

Rock climbing looks fun but dangerous. No fear as there are indoor rock climbing gyms where you can feel the rush of climbing the side of a mountain while in safety restraints. There are plenty of places around that have in-door rock climbing. It can be challenging and entertaining as a sense of accomplishment washes over you when you complete a climb. Together you can feel like you can achieve anything.

Tips to remember:

- Make sure your date is not afraid of heights and would enjoy this type of activity.
- Many spas, gyms or recreational centers have indoor rock climbing.
- Be supportive and if she is reticent, spur her on. Tell her you are there with her the whole way. And, if you let her start her climb before you, then you will more than likely enjoy the view.

F. Gym / Yoga

Mariann admits, working out for her is something she does for a reason and not because she loves doing it. Sharon can't live a week without doing her yoga class. We both have friends who are gym rats and are most at home when working out. It's good for a couple to stay healthy together and working out in a gym or taking a yoga class together is a perfect opportunity to do that. Trainers will tell you, the best way to keep to an exercise schedule is to work out with a friend!

Tips to remember:

- A good date if she is into yoga even if you are not. You will enjoy seeing how flexible she is.
- Many spas, gyms, yoga studios or recreational centers have yoga classes.
- Bring water. Have fun.

Suggestions and information:

- If your date is a real yoga lover, take her to a local yoga retreat. For example, The Kripalu center in Massachusetts, *www.kripalu.org*, is a great place for an hour's class or a full weekend retreat.
- Want to find a yoga center in your area, try: *www.retreatfinder.com*

Go stretch your imagination ... and your body!

G. Fruit Farms

Come spring or summer, fruit farms are a great reason to get outside and enjoy bonding with Mother Earth. You can pick fruit, have a lazy day, and can appreciate the picturesque surroundings while picking fruit you find succulent. Instead of going to the supermarket for strawberries or blueberries, pick them yourself. When you get home, use your freshly picked fruit to make a delicious dessert together. If it is fall, you can go apple and pumpkin picking, go on a hayride, get lost in a corn maze, have apple cider and donuts and picnic with some sandwiches.

Tips to remember:
- Do a little research on Google or Yahoo to find a fruit farm, pumpkin or apple picking farm near you. If you are going to more than one, just work out the logistics.
- Many places serve food. Call ahead to find out if the farm includes a food stand or cozy cafe. Want some privacy? Pack a picnic basket.
- Let the day be carefree.
- This is a great opportunity to go back to your place and make a dessert together. There is a recipe for **Strawberries Romanoff** in the back of this book. Google recipes for blueberry pie, strawberry shortcake or apple crisp! Then, get cozy on the couch feasting on your very fresh dessert.

It will be a fun day to relax and connect under blue skies and a warm sun!

H. Tennis

Maybe you will find out if this is a love match when you play tennis. Take your passion to the courts and unleash some friendly competition as you battle it out for the game. You'll be invigorated afterward. OK, so if you are both not Wimbledon caliber, then just delight in running around *attempting* to hit the ball. A little silliness is always good when you know you are not as good as your opponent. You may work up an appetite for — I will leave that to your imagination. But, after the game you can hit the showers — and maybe together!

Tips to remember:
- Make sure she wants to play tennis.
- Does she have a racket? If not, you can pick up an inexpensive one at a sports store, or rent one at the tennis center.
- Don't get carried away with the competition. Keep it light and lively.

I. Skiing / Snowmobiling / Tubing

Enjoy the cold and speeding out of control down a hill? Or maneuvering a machine over bumps and snowy terrain? Then hitting the slopes to go skiing, snowboarding, tubing or snowmobiling is a perfect way to spend the day. The thrill-seeker in you will relish the spirit of the day as you warm your hearts together in the stark cold. Hit the lodge afterward and snuggle on the couch with a hot toddy in front of the fireplace.

Tips to remember:
- Make sure she can ski or would enjoy snowmobiling or tubing.
- A simple Google or Yahoo search will list options in your area.
- Be sensitive if she is hesitant at first. Look out after her to make sure she is OK. After a few minutes, we're sure she'll seem like a pro.

If you want to make it even more romantic, get a room with a view!

J. Ice Skating

Grab your gal and go Ice Skating. Take her hand and swirl her around the rink guiding her past wobbly skaters and the really bad skaters who land on their butts. Laugh and feel free as you circle the rink together. When the cold gets too much and her nose looks like Rudolph's, step in from the cold and sit rink side or at a lodge fireplace to sip hot cocoa and nuzzle to get warm.

Tips to remember:
- Make sure she is into skating.
- If she is not very good, use it as an opportunity to hold her hand and keep her close. Make sure not to leave her crawling along the railing while you are skating circles around her.
- Be sensitive if she is cold and needs to warm up. We're confident you can warm her up quickly!

It is a light hearted and romantic outing that will keep you both smiling!

19 Seal The Deal Date
($ to $$$$$ / ♥♥♥ to ♥♥♥♥♥)

This is it. You want to serenade your lady and this is the night you quash any question marks about where the relationship is headed. It will let her know she's special and set the stage for falling in love, if that's your goal. This is the time to do something that is different or thoughtful. You will need more planning skills here, so really think about your budget and what will resonate with what your lady likes. The goal here is to make her know that being with you is fun and exciting, that you will always take care of her and that you are there for her.

DATE	COST	ROMANCE
Five Star All The Way	$$$ - $$$$$	♥♥♥♥♥
Up Up and Away	$ - $$$	♥♥♥♥
Dining Decadence In Your Own Home	$ - $$$$	♥♥♥

Things to consider:
- This is full on romance and a date to let her know you love her.
- A lot of planning and logistics may be required.
- Expensive. This means you are serious.
- Requires listings of Plays, Opera, Bands, Restaurants and Bars/Lounges/Clubs at your destination.
- Create a memory with love notes or a memento.

Things you may need:
Note cards, memento, picnic set up (basket, food, drinks), listing for plays and venues for entertainment, food, home décor items, champagne, flowers, iPod/speakers, equipment to play movie or your own video, gift bag of sexy goodies, dessert, lingerie, CD.

A. Five Star All The Way

With this date you will possibly spend a good deal of money so make sure you can afford it. If things are a bit tight, we will offer budget conscious options. You have to ask yourself what your girlfriend loves to do or what she considers a "treat" or something she always wanted to do but hasn't been able to. For example, does she love opera? Is there a play she has been dying to see? A rock band that is touring that hasn't been together in while? An experience she has read about and is curious to try? Once you start answering these kinds of questions, you can craft a 5-star date.

Tips to remember:
- Ask your gal what she'd most like to do, or where she'd like to go.
- A play or an opera are great ideas. Having a limo pick her up with you and champagne waiting inside is definitely 5-star.
- Treat her like a Queen. Hold open the door. Help her in and out of the car. Attend to every detail of the evening.
- Remember the moment with a CD of the opera or musical you see.
- Make sure to pick a restaurant with a romantic ambience that she will enjoy and where you can flirt and talk and flirt. Restaurants with fireplaces are always romantic.

If you want to amp up the evening, arrange to stay over at a nice hotel where you can continue your special night out. If you do stay over, you can always go to the hotel and get ready there and then head out to your evening. The logistics of that is up to you. If you do stay over, make sure to arrange some flowers, or a nice box waiting on the bed that holds some sexy lingerie or jewelry. If you have the funds, then rent out a restaurant or museum or botanical garden for a dinner just for you two. Have a violinist serenade you. Or, hire a singer who can provide the background for dinner and dancing.

Suggestions and information:
- Fireplaces in lounges, bars and restaurants are always cozy. Go to *www.zagat.com* or *www.yelp.com* for ideas and reviews.
- If you are not done and want to have more fun, find a pretty wine bar, or eclectic dessert bar. If you want something with a little more vibe, maybe a champagne bar. An example of an edgy champagne bar is the Bubble Lounge (*www.bubblelounge.com*) in New York City and San Francisco.
- Google to find great places in your area. Aside from Yahoo travel, here are some websites to check out about wine and champagne bars:

> *www.foodandwine.com/slideshows/americas-best-bars*
> *www.worldsbestbars.com*
> *www.travel.yahoo.com/ideas/America-s-best-wine-bars.html*

Now, if funds are tighter, then nix the hotel or use some hotel reward points if you have them. Don't use a limo, but make sure you help your lady into and out of the car and hold the door. Do all the gentlemanly things your parents taught you. Have a CD or flower or small gift ready. Do you need center orchestra seats? Perhaps not. Maybe you get mezzanine seats or go to see an indy band that she loves. So, you can still take your special lady out on the town for a memorable night out that will see her running into your arms!

B. Up Up and Away ...

Women love excursions that are original. By planning an outing that is different, it tells your girlfriend that you thought carefully about every detail. This is very sexy to ladies. Women relish knowing their boyfriend thought carefully about making them feel special. If your lady is not afraid of heights and has a sense of adventure, plan a Hot Air Balloon ride and get swept away by the exhilarating experience as you fly together at low altitudes over a pretty countryside. It may be a bit scary, but you can hold her close and make her feel safe. Take photos and capture a once in a lifetime moment. You can mark the outing with a special memento like a helium filled balloon or cute little balloon earrings. If you really want to be sweet, write her a love note (on a card with a hot air balloon perhaps) to make her heart soar.

Tips to remember:
• Make sure your girlfriend is not afraid of heights.
• Know if a hot air balloon would be exciting to her or is totally off her bucket list.
• Make your lady love feel safe.
• Write her a love note and read while you are up in the air or when back on the ground.
• You can let her know about this date or make it a surprise.
• Create a memory of the day/experience with a memento.
• *Don't forget* your camera.

Once your feet are back on the ground, you will both be giggly and invigorated for sure. As your adrenaline subsides, share a picnic basket and relax and cuddle on a blanket under the skies you just visited. It will be a memorable day for sure.

Suggestions and information:
- Go to the internet and search for local venues.
- Try a website called Xperiencedays (*www.xperiencedays.com*) for different adventures and hot air ballooning is an option and is broken down by state! You'll find options for many other types of interactive experiences here too, so you can plan your own original adventure date. And you can buy gift certificates too!

C. Dining Decadence In Your Own Home

Some of Sharon's favorite dates have been intimate meals at home. Do you like to cook? If yes, plan a delectable and sensual meal for just the two of you. If not, pick a great restaurant and have it catered. Think of dinner as setting a stage for intimacy. This date is meant to be an orgasm for your tastebuds! You have to give thought to the ambience, the meal and what to do. If you don't have the time but have the funds to spend, you can use the services of an event planner or someone who specializes in organizing or planning intimate gatherings. For example, in the Los Angeles area there is an interior design and event planning company *"... By Michelle"* that has capitalized on this niche market. They can stage your date by designing, planning and coordinating the date and ambience for a special evening in your own home. What a great idea and perfect for those busy guys on the go who need a little assistance.

Tips to remember:
- Set the mood of the evening. Have the setting be aesthetically pleasing.
- Set the table with a cloth and nice tableware and glassware adorned with flowers or long stemmed candles. Ask a friend to help with setting a table.
- Know if your date is allergic to any foods. You don't want to end your date in the emergency room!
- Have plenty of candles to set a warm glow. Have no or very little

lighting other than candles. Use fragrant oils to please her sense of smell, but don't go overboard.

- Make her favorite meal or all appetizers you can both sample. Or, just cater your delectable delights!
- Underscore the evening with some slow and sensual background music.
- Don't talk about everyday things. Bring up sexy topics, titillating conversation and flirt. Set the mood for a night of passion
- Get a professional to set the stage for you.

Plan your menu to appeal to her sense of taste and make sure all the food is succulent and decadent. Your goal is about setting a sexy night for your lady and making her feel desired and sexy. For dessert, have some Strawberries Romanoff with whipped cream. Perhaps you can have more fun with the whipped cream later on in the evening. After dinner, slow dance and have everything you say, eat and do build up anticipation for a steamy night in the bedroom!

Suggestions and information:

- For table settings and accessories, you can go to Pier One, Bed Bath & Beyond or Crate & Barrel. An assistant would be more than happy to help you.
- You can get information on how to set a romantic table at: *www.ehow.com/how_2338210_set-table-romantic-dinner.html*
- Find out how to make Strawberries Romanoff in the Sexy Recipe section in the back of this book. It takes 10 minutes!!
- Check out a great and novel company, "*...By Michelle*" which not only does interior design but plans events large and small. Michelle has capitalized on a niche market and can plan and coordinate an event as small as an intimate meal for you and your lady. Mariann attended a larger dinner gathering planned by "*...By Michelle*" and it was awesome! The website is: *www.by-michelle.com*
- Need help with video preparation? In the New York / New Jersey area I have used *www.motofoto.com* or *www.rgibs.com*.

Once dessert is over, you might want to break out her favorite movie or, if you have the time or talent, you might want to make your own cute, funny or touching video of yourselves as a couple. You can even add text and music. Have the video celebrate her light and spirit and the joy she has brought to your life. A homemade movie will be a home run and she will be all over you. Remember, it's all about appreciating and celebrating her and showing her how special she is to you!

20 Special Occasion ($$ to $$$$ / ♥♥♥ to ♥♥♥♥)

Life is full of occasions we want to commemorate or acknowledge. It's all about creating a memory that will last forever. Underscoring a special occasion with a celebration or unique and memorable outing is a perfect way to show your girlfriend that you want to make her and this moment as special as you possibly can.

DATE	COST	ROMANCE
Let Her Decide!	$$ - $$$$	♥♥♥♥
Dinner Cruise – Ahoy Matey!	$$ - $$$	♥♥♥♥
Go To An Astrologer – It's In The Stars	$$ - $$$	♥♥♥

Things to consider:

• This date is intended to underscore a special occasion. It's more sweet and romantic than sensual/sexy.
• This date involves a little research and planning.
• Make sure your girlfriend is OK with boats on water and is not offended by astrologers.
• If you give her free reign to plan a date, just go with it and have fun.

Things you may need:

Dining Guide (Zagat or internet), dinner / venue reservations, memento for memory or nice gift (jewelry), astrologer, scroll, rose/flowers.

A. Let Her Decide!

One way to put off having to plan a date is to make it a challenge for your girl. Give her a budget and tell her to plan whatever she wants for anything you are celebrating. Genius, right? She can plan as she sees fit, or you can work on it as a team. Some women are good planners and love to plan dates and take control. If your gal is one of them, then handing her the reigns is a treat for her and a pass for you! Be warned — whatever she comes up with, just smile and enjoy it!

Key things to remember:
- Make this fun for her. You can plan the date together and both have fun too!
- Give her a budget and tell her to plan what she wants.
- Let yourself enjoy whatever has come into her imagination. Who knows, she might go a bit above and beyond in her planning and that is her surprise to you. Don't complain, go happily and have a blast.

B. Dinner Cruise — Ahoy Ahoy!

A Dinner Cruise means boat, food, drinks, water, pretty scenery, music, dancing and moonlit skies with your special lady. It's a perfect recipe for a great night out. Whether it is a dinner cruise on the river or a gambling river boat on the Mississippi or the Hornblower Cruises out of Newport Beach, CA (dinner and dancing) try to find a cruise that tours you past pretty scenery, provides a good meal and has music and dancing. I bet you will step off the boat wanting to repeat that voyage soon. Inside festivities becoming a bit too much? No problem, stroll out on the deck, whisper some sweet nothings in your date's ear and sneak a few kisses while the moonlit sky provides the back drop to a very romantic evening.

Tips to remember:
- Make sure your date likes boats and is not prone to sea sickness.
- Make her feel special by bringing some lively fun to the evening along with a lot of romance.
- Give your gal a reason to get dressed up and look sexy! If there is a special occasion to acknowledge, then give her an appropriate gift. For example, did she just get a promotion? Then perhaps a gold plate inscribed with her name on it which she can place on her desk.

Suggestions and information:
- Use Google, Yahoo, or Bing to find dinner cruises in your area.
- For a gambling river boat cruise, there are many and some with a hotel for overnight. This link provides some good insight: *www.ehow.com/list_5976902_louisiana-riverboat-casinos.html*
- If in New York City, take a dinner cruise on the Hudson that circles the Statue of Liberty and Brooklyn Bridge. It is stunning and romantic. It's

the three-hour tour except without Gilligan, the Skipper and the gang. And if you do go a drift, you'll probably just wind up in New Jersey! Try, *www.worldyacht.com/site/home.aspx*

• In California, look up Hornblower Cruises, *www.hornblower.com/hce/home*
  In Florida, try: *victorycasinocruises.com/*

C. Go To An Astrologer — It's In The Stars

What's your sign? Ever curious how the alignment of the stars impacts your life? Your career? You love life? We don't follow astrology like a religion, but Mariann and Sharon are intrigued by it. As a Taurean and Sagittarian respectively, Mariann and Sharon are surprised at how astrology website descriptions of them are accurate. Also, some signs are more compatible than others. Want to know more about your sun sign? We have found *www.astrologyzone.com* is a wonderful site. And, it will even tell you how you match with the other signs. In addition, it tells you what a specific sign likes in romance which can make a great framework for a date. It's a fun way to craft a celebratory outing — and could open the door to a lively discussion of your respective signs' traits.

Tips to remember:

• Make sure your date is into or at least amused by astrology. If not, try another date.
• Plan the date around what astrology sites or astrologers suggest that your dates' sign likes to do and how to be romanced. For example, does her sign crave luxurious relaxation? If yes, take her to a spa. Is her sign into adventure? Take her zip lining or to an amusement park. Is her sign curious and intellectual? Take her to a museum.
• Start the date by visiting an astrologer to get a reading. Most astrologers will do a couples reading. This can run $50-$250 depending on who you go to and for how long.
• Afterward, give her a scroll or card with some details of the date and how it ties into her sign or your celebration. Whatever you use, keep the theme of anything you give her directed towards astrology, her sign or the positive traits of her sign!

Suggestions and information:

- Go to *www.astrologyzone.com* to get info on your dates' astrological sign. It has a section called "Life & Love" where you can find gift ideas, how to seduce your love, stress busters and vacation tips — all for your gal's sign. Use this to build the framework of your date.
- Go to an astrologer. They charge based on time or reputation. In New York City, Mariann has visited Shelley Ackerman at *www.karmicrelief.com* who she met at a writing conference. There, Shelley taught a class in how your astrological sign affects your writing.
- Outside New York, ask around or contact Karmicrelief or Astrologyzone for a recommendation in your area. Some do over the phone readings, but an in-person visit is part of the fun of the date.

Underscore how the traits of her astrological sign highlights her success or the foundation of your celebration. Framing a date in a different manner with a theme makes your celebration just a bit more memorable. If you can carry the theme through the night, all the better!

21 Spice Up Your Dating Life
($ to $$$ / ♥♥♥ to ♥♥♥♥)

You don't want your relationship, life, sex life or romantic life to get stale and boring. It won't be fun and sexy if you and your partner don't put the effort into ensuring it remains hot and sizzling. OK, so is it going to be sizzling hot every night? Probably not. If it is, then good for you! Too often people don't stay connected to each other. This happens with friendship and lovers. The only way to prevent a void from happening or distance from growing between you is to make sure that you always make time for each other. Remember to stay in tune with each other and always find new reasons to fall in love. Reconnect to the reasons you fell in love in the first place. Remind each other, with sincerity, that you do love each other and why. As great as it is to be sexy and romantic, it is also fabulous to be sweet.

DATE	COST	ROMANCE
Sexy Shopping	$ - $$$	♥♥♥♥♥
Food and Chocolate Show	$ - $$$	♥♥♥
Pick A Fantasy – Any Fantasy	$ - $$$	♥♥♥♥
Massage For Two	$ - $$	♥♥♥♥
50 Shades Of Erotic	$ - $$$	♥♥♥♥♥

Things to consider:
- These dates can be very sexual in nature. So, unless you are intimate with this person, move on to another date idea.
- These dates can be very low cost if you want them to be.
- Make sure your date is not offended by erotic adult toys or going to such places.
- These dates are good to have fun with. They really play up your flirting and getting your sexy on!
- Some dates need a bit more planning than others.

Things you may need:

Listing of food shows, adult toy shops, adult toys, massage oils, robe, candles, erotic desserts from a bakery, wine/bubbly, velvet bag, paper for writing out fantasies, food/snacks that could be theme oriented, imagination, sexy negligée, massage therapy class.

It's good to keep it saucy and spicy. Feel free to let your imagination run wild and have some fun with it. The couple that laughs together, in or out of the bedroom, stays together!

A. Sexy Shopping

You read right — sexy shopping! It's important to keep the romance alive in a relationship. Erotic is good too! I am sure there is a store in your area that sells items that can add some spice to the bedroom. Why not go shopping together and pick out what you like or for each other. Whether it is massage oils, a French maid outfit, edible underwear, body paints, handcuffs or something a bit more extreme, roam the store having fun figuring out what to buy and try first. In the store, you're adding a bit of anticipation to a steamy night and foreplay with a lot of hot flirting. After building an appetite, go to a chocolate and wine bar, or head back to your place where you can feast on some erotic desserts.

Tips to remember:
- Make sure she does not mind shopping for sexy toys.
- Make sure you pay unless she wants to buy something for you!
- Flirt up a storm. You're in a sex shop, get racy and sexy. Make it a really hot night!
- If you do go out afterwards to a wine or coffee bar, be discreet if you decide to look at your purchases! Others could be jealous.

If you go back to your place, make sure you have planned to keep it a naughty night. Order some erotic desserts from a bakery and have them waiting along with the beverage of your lady's choice (coffee, soda, champagne, wine, after dinner liqueur). Just make sure you have a choice for her.

Suggestions and information:
- Go to your favorite search engine and type in *sex shops* or *adult toys* or *sex toys* and the city you live in and an array of options will be listed.
- If you live in New York City, the Pink Pussycat in the west village

or the Kiki de Montparnasse (*www.kikidm.com*) in Soho are common destinations for couples who want to find sexy toys and lingerie.

- For sexy lingerie, try Fredericks of Hollywood (*www.fredericks.com*). On the Upper East Side in New York City, visit Myla (*www.myla.com*) for some beautiful sleepwear!
- In the L.A. area? Try the Pleasure Chest (*www.thepleasurechest.com*), Hustler (*www.hustlerstore.com*), Romantix (*www.romantixon-line.com*), or Agent Provocatuer (*www.agentprovocatuer.com*).
- If you don't want to go out to an adult store, then shop on-line. Check out My Pleasure at *www.mypleasure.com* which is an on-line adult toy store where you and your partner can find every type of X to XXX rated sensual products.
- For a chocolate and wine bar, try Ayza in New York City. Again, just search on-line for chocolate and wine in your area and you'll find many venues.
- Need an erotic bakery? Google, Bing and Yahoo are your friends – use them. But, here are a few links that can help as well. This company has erotic bakery items: *theeroticbakery.com/* or this company has locations all over the country and they ship: *www.eroticbakery.net/erotic_cakes_usa_locations.html*

After you have feasted on some sugary delights and are nestled into each other's arms, you can continue the sensual evening where *other desserts* may be in store!

B. Food and Chocolate Show

Are you a foodie? Is your girlfriend? If yes, what better way to romance her than with some scrumptious food or savory chocolate? You can wander the floor of a food show and sample an array of gourmet delights. It will be pleasurable tasting so many different foods, perhaps paired with some zingy wines. And if there is a chocolate show (like the one in New York every fall) then all the better! Chocolate is an aphrodisiac! The Food Network sponsors Wine & Food Festivals in New York and Florida. You and your date could rub elbows with your favorite celebrity chefs too!

Tips to remember:
- This is not an expensive date and can be a lot of fun.

- Research the food or chocolate show and buy tickets in advance.
- If your gal absolutely adores those Swiss Champagne truffles – go ahead, get her a box!
- You can end your evening with a drink if you want to make it last longer!

Suggestions and information:
- Just search on-line for *Food* or *Chocolate Show*. You can put in your area. Many search results are old, so make sure they are for the current year.
- Here is a website that lists food shows revolving around sweets: *www.tradefairdates.com/Trade-Shows-for-Sweets-Chocolate-Y326-S1.html*

Your lady will love this date. You can't go wrong with great food and yummy sweets! Perhaps you can pick up some chocolate syrup, whipped cream and cherries and use them later on in the evening — just a suggestion!

C. Pick A Fantasy — Any Fantasy

Everyone has fantasies. It's natural. And role playing can be exciting and healthy for a relationship. Plan an entertaining and steamy night in. Buy a sexy game or Kama Sutra flash cards and have a blast trying the positions. Another more personal idea is for each to come up with five fantasies and write them on individual pieces of paper. First, have her place her fantasies in a Fantasy Bag. Then, you reach into the bag of *her* fantasies and pick one to act out or plan. Next, put your fantasies into the bag. Have your gal pick one of *your* fantasies to act out or plan. Act out these fantasies then and there or, if they're more elaborate, take time for planning and logistics. For example, your fantasy could be that your car breaks down and you are alone on a dark road and a stranger (aka: girlfriend) comes by to help you. The instant connection is too much to contain so you have sex under stars or in the car (hopefully you have a roomy car!). Maybe she drives you to a nearby hotel where the passion you can't contain is expressed in a long night of love making. Whatever the fantasy, revel in the thrill of your imagination and hers.

Tips to remember:
- This is an intimate date. You are sharing something deep. Make sure you are both ready for it.

- Bring a sense of fun and frivolity to the evening.
- If you want to change it up, then have a theme for the evening (Arabian Nights, Bohemian, Mad Men 1960s, France 1940s). Whatever it is, really play it up in ambience, food, music, and what you wear. Have fun with it.
- You might build up an appetite, so have food ready.
- If anything makes her uncomfortable, then respect her and stop.
- The idea of putting selections into a bag can apply to dates, restaurants, vacations and other activities.

Be as specific as possible on a theme, the time of night, what the person is wearing, what they smell like or how you want the fantasy to happen. Is there a specific statement you want said? Are there any props you want incorporated? Think of it as theater where you have to set the stage and act the part. It can be saucy, sexy and hot.

D. Massage For Two

The human touch is comforting and sensual. A massage can be relaxing and erotic. Mariann personally loves a massage and jokes she might like to marry a masseur some day! But, the sense of touch is very powerful. It can make you feel so many things. Giving a massage requires technique. Sure, you can give a deep tissue massage because the lower back is a bit strained. But giving a sensual massage with fragrant oils and really synching your body to your lovers can be electrifying. It can bond you in a way that you can do best without words.

Tips to remember:
- Investigate a massage seminar or a class and sign up yourself and your girlfriend. Try an adult education class or a health center.
- Practice on each other. Who said homework wasn't fun? We're sure you'll get an "A."
- Don't have time for a class, seminar or actual instruction? Get a DVD on massage technique and test your skills out on each other.

Really want to get into the massage mood? Get matching soft cozy spa robes and slippers. Light scented candles for ambience. Get some essential oils then set out on a sensory journey. If the massage has a happy ending — well, that's up to you!

E. 50 Shades Of Erotic

With the blockbuster popularity of "50 Shades Of Gray", more people are becoming curious about and experimenting with their sexuality. Granted there have been a few book burnings for some to garner their own attention and capitalize on the publicity of such salacious topics. But the fact remains, many people are exploring practices that fall outside of what they have been doing for years in order to spice up their marriages or relationships. Sales of toys, books and videos at adult shops are soaring and it has been a stellar year for many of these stores. Also increasing are courses people or couples can take about sex, intimacy and other alternate lifestyle practices. If you and your gal really want to step outside the box and explore this together, then you can find classes that will provide instruction.

We will caution you here. This is serious. You do not want to damage your relationship or introduce something that will compromise it or make the other person uncomfortable. The overwhelming expert advice is that you both have to be open to this. The most important element is communication. You must talk about how you feel, how things make you feel, what your limits are, and what is OK or not. You each must respect if the other wants to stop, and have ground rules on how to approach this. So whether you decide to open your relationship to others or incorporate equipment or practices that are not considered normal sexual practice, then that is up to you. It is imperative this be consensual and that you implement strong communication, as jealousy can and will rear its ugly head. If you don't, you risk losing an important relationship. Several places have instructional or informative classes on these alternate lifestyles and practices and how you communicate as a couple navigating this new lifestyle.

Tips you remember on this date:
- This is very serious. You must both have talked about this before you propose such a class or change in practice.
- If you are both on board, do not just jump in idly. Find classes that give you an introduction to the lifestyle or practice so you know what you are getting yourself into.
- Slowly figure out what it is you want to do and take all necessary safety precautions to ensure no one is hurt emotionally or physically.
- If you and your girl are more private about your sexuality, search on-

line for websites that offer insight into what you'd like to explore. The research alone could lead to a steamy evening.

Suggestions and information:

- You can find a reference to adult shops in the "Sexy Shopping" date. Also try Romantix (*www.romantixon-line.com*) in L.A. or Hustler (*www.hustlerstore.com*).
- The Pleasure Chest in L.A. is also a popular adult store plus, they also have and are associated with classes.
- Search listings for your interests and your location and you will find something to get you educated. You can also call the adult shops near you and ask for any referrals or recommendations to any informative classes.

Tread carefully with the one you love and make sure you don't have 50 Shades of Regret.

22 Summer Fun ($ to $$$ / ♥ to ♥♥♥)

Summer Fun is almost obligatory. Warm weather, sun, and late sunsets create the perfect recipe to have a blast. So, take advantage and go enjoy yourselves! That's mandatory. Now go!

DATE	COST	ROMANCE
Mini Golf	$ - $$	♥♥
Country Fair	$	♥♥
Amusement Park	$ - $$	♥♥♥
Beach Volleyball	$	♥
Arcade	$ - $$	♥
Racetrack	$ - $$$	♥♥
Horseback Riding	$	♥♥
Fishing	$	♥
Shakespeare In The Park	$	♥♥♥
Water Park	$ - $$	♥

Things to consider:
- These dates are for people who are in various stages of a relationship.
- There is very little planning except perhaps for a simple internet search.
- Meant to be a "get to know" date or a simple but romantic date. You can ramp up the romance whenever you want.
- These dates are fun, relaxing, and casual and won't break the bank.
- Don't put stress on yourself to make the date more than what it is — an enjoyable date in nice weather with the girl you like beside you!

Things you may need:
Backpack of supplies, bathing suit, towels, extra change of clothing, money for arcade games and racetrack betting.

A. Mini Golf
Many beach and vacation towns have Mini Golf. Take a day and head to the beach for a day of swimming. Afterward, head over to the mini golf course

and challenge each other to get a hole in one. Most people enjoy a playful round of mini golf and the challenge of hitting a ball through a miniature windmill. Not near a beach? That's OK. Most states have vacation areas with mini golf. Make it interesting, have a *friendly* wager based on who wins or who gets a hole in one. It can be as G-rated, or sexy as like!

B. Country Fair

What's more American than a Country Fair? Step back to a simpler time when entertainment was innocent and pure. Go on a carnival ride. Try to win a prize for your gal. Eat a super greasy hamburger, foot long hotdog or cotton candy with abandon. Play horseshoe, ride a pony or go square dancing. This will be a fun day to find pleasure in the simple things. Get your face painted or listen to some good 'ole country music and keep your foot tapping to the beat! You might wish that it was 1872 and feel nostalgic — well, until your cell phone rings and brings you back to reality.

If you and your date want to go further back to an even simpler time than that, look for a local summer Renaissance Faire. Here, you can go back to the time of Robin Hood and his Merry Men and spend the day with knights, damsels, and street performers. You can even dress in period costume and play along with the performers.

Suggestions and information:
• Point your browser to *www.renfaire.com* for listings of many Fairs operating in the U.S.A.
• Google State Fairs to find one that is local to you.

C. Amusement Park

Amusement Parks are blissfully entertaining. Sometimes, we forget this. Six Flags, Universal and Disney are but a few to consider. Remember your high school senior trip to an Amusement Park? Go back to being 18 again. Enjoy the rides. Kiss passionately on the ferris wheel. Squeal with happiness as the roller coaster soars around scary turns. Laugh as you play bumper cars. Walk hand in hand around the park. Take in some great shows. Be a kid again and enjoy every moment of it, and if you feel like skipping – go ahead!

Suggestions and information:

- Want to know more about Six Flags, check out their locations: *www.sixflags.com/national/index.aspx*
- If you want to know all amusement parks listing by states, this link might prove helpful: *themeparks.about.com/cs/usparks/l/blparksbystate.htm*

D. Beach Volleyball

If you love the beach and being athletic, then hurry down to the sand, set up your camp, then get that volleyball and have some aerobic fun diving into the sand to save that point. If you want to make it sexy, agree to kiss after each point. Or, whoever wins gets a massage from the loser or treats to some oysters and champagne after the sun goes down. You will get some sun, exercise, and have a truly relaxed and carefree day!

E. Arcade

Sharon says she loves arcades and has since she was a kid. Who doesn't love skeet ball or being a pinball wizard? Earn a stuffed teddy bear for your lady by winning the ball toss. Hopping into a helicopter or race car simulator can provide hours of pure delight. You'll forget your troubles and just have a fun-filled good time! Play an enthusiastic game of air hockey and when you are done, redeem your many tickets for cute trinkets that can be a memory of your eventful day together! What could be a better date than that?

Suggestions and information:

- Dave & Busters is a chain of restaurants with indoor arcades that are fun for kids and adults. Several locations also have pool tables and 3D rides. For a great time, check out their website: *www.daveandbusters.com/default.aspx*
- If you want to know all arcades in the US by state, this link is just what you need: *www.arcadepages.info/*

F. Racetrack

And … you're off … to the races! Most racetracks have great races, food and drinks. Learn how to bet as you make your wagers on a sure winner.

You don't want to lose your house, but definitely have some laughs making your bets. Go early for dinner and enjoy a tasty meal. Relax with a few drinks, all the while watching the many horses running for the finish line. You'll get home and giggle at how much fun you had. You'll think, *"we gotta do that again."* A racetrack date gives a different angle on just going for dinner. It makes the date more interesting, and who doesn't love a friendly wager? We both do!

Suggestions and information:
- For a list of the Horse Racing Tracks in the US by state, go to: *www.officialusa.com/stateguides/horseracingtracks/index.html*

G. Horseback Riding

Horses are often viewed as romantic and a symbol of early America. They remind us of pioneers who had the resilience and commitment to working for a better life. Horses are beautiful. Give your lady the gift of sitting atop a stunning animal as she cajoles it to carry her through a park or woods or even along a beach. If you or your gal are animal lovers, this is a great opportunity to feel at one with these lovely creatures. Once you're done, plan a nice picnic and enjoy a day out amidst a pretty, lush green setting.

Suggestions and information:
- If you are looking for horse rentals or horseback riding by state, try this link: *www.horserentals.com/horses.html*
- Another useful site for everything horse related: *www.horseshowcentral.com/horse_stables.php*
- If you are looking for a dude ranch, riding lessons or stables, use this link: *www.horseandtravel.com/*

H. Fishing

Enjoy seafood? Take a fishing boat out, throw in your line and wait. As the sun beats down and the boat rocks gently with the waves, before long you will be yelling, *"Net! Net!"* as you reel in your deadliest catch. If you don't throw the fish back, then have your fish filleted at the dock. At home, after getting your land legs, pour a great Riesling and grill your catch with some tasty vegetables as you relax on your porch enjoying the labors of your hard work. Want something a bit less structured and more low key? No problem. Hit a lake, get a row boat, pack some snacks, and row to a cove or to the middle of the lake – throw in a line and see what happens. If nothing is biting, take the opportunity to float and perhaps read some poetry to your lady love while you wait.

I. Shakespeare In The Park

In the mood for a little culture and an English accent? Well, head to a Medieval Festival where you can roam around feeling like you were transported back in time. Play chess on the lawn with strangers or your lady. Buy handmade candles. Snack on sugary and carb-heavy delights. Inquire if there's a Shakespearian play in the park, and go set up front and center with a perfect view of the action. Whether it's a drama or comedy, you will be entertained for sure! This is a great way to spend a wonderful day and evening outdoors.

Suggestions and information:

- Want to combine Shakespeare with a visit to a B & B, this site can help: *bbbard.com/index.php*
- For a listing of Shakespeare Festivals and theaters by state, try this link: *www.shakespearefellowship.org/linksfestivals.htm*
- In Canada? Bard on the Beach in Vancouver is Canada's largest Shakespeare Festival: *en.wikipedia.org/wiki/Bard_on_the_Beach* and *www.bardonthebeach.org* They perform June through September.
- Another listing of Shakespeare theater companies and festivals by name is: *shakespeare.palomar.edu/festivals.htm*
- Looking for drama and theater outdoors? Try this link: *www.outdoordrama.org/about/*

J. Water Park

Interrupt the hot rays of sun that hit your back as you jump into a pool or travel the log flume or take a raft ride down a wild river. Scream with pure joy as you speed down an extra-long slide. Splash around in the water like a fish and cool off. This is a day where you don't think of anything but having a cool time and which ride will be next! We guarantee you will not be disappointed. And, if your lady is wearing a bikini, then the sights just got even better. Like we've said, who could ask for a better day?

Suggestions and information:

- Listing of waterparks by state:
themeparks.about.com/cs/waterparks/l/blwaterparksst.htm (just click on your state)
- This is a good site for simple listings by state with links to parks:
www.ultimatewaterpark.com/waterparks/parks_by_state.php
- Another listing of waterparks by state is:
www.waterparks.com/default.asp (note: for states, type out the name of the state not the abbreviation)

23 Theme Date ($ to $$$$ / ♥ to ♥♥♥♥)

We find theme dates and evenings special. That's the theater person in us. But, it gives you and your lady a chance to play along and really get into the mood and mode of the theme.

DATE	COST	ROMANCE
Sailing	$$ - $$$$	♥♥♥♥
Murder Mystery	$$ - $$$	♥♥
Act Like A Tourist	$ - $$$	♥♥
Sporting Events	$$ - $$$	♥♥
Make Wine Together	$$ - $$$	♥♥♥
Haunted House	$	♥
Christmas Light Tour	$	♥♥
The 007 Date	$$ - $$$$	♥♥♥ - ♥♥♥♥

Things to consider:
- These dates involve varying levels of cost and planning.
- They are romantic, fun and spontaneous. You can increase the romance on any one of these dates. Just bring flowers, write her a love note or give a memento of the event.
- These dates are for people who are in new relationships and those in serious relationships.

Things you may need:

Backpack of supplies, water, snacks, travel (depending on how serious you get with visiting a haunted house or seeing a Christmas light display).

A. Sailing

Sailing! This is a great idea! The execution of this date can take a few forms. You can go out on a sailboat for the day or, you can take sailing lessons. If you just want to have the cool breeze in your hair and don't want to be a "student" forget the lessons. Have you talked with your girlfriend about taking sailing lessons? If you love the water, learning, boats and the sun, then sailing is for you. It's a sport of thought and analysis. This past summer, Sharon took sailing lessons and had a blast! She wished she had been dating someone at the time as it would have been a great weekend and bonding experience. We would love to find someone with whom we had *our thing*, something we could do together and that we were passionate about. We think Sailing can be that thing…

Tips to remember:
- Sailing lessons are not cheap, so make sure this is something your girlfriend wants to do.
- Take water and snacks for a day out on the water. Don't forget supplies like sun glasses, sun tan lotion and a towel. Oh yea, and remember to pack a change of clothes.
- Want to make more of an outing? Stay in a hotel. Go back to the hotel, take a shower and hit the town for some good food and good times!
- A simple internet search will list sailing schools near you.

Bring the idea up to your lady or if you know she would love to go sailing then make it a surprise. Take her out for seafood, and then have a gift bag with cute little things that are sailing themed. Write up a gift certificate or card that tells her what you have planned and present it over dinner. It really will give her something to look forward to doing with you.

B. Murder Mystery

The purpose of a themed date is to take what you normally do and step it up or make it different. Instead of just going to dinner, why not go to a Murder Mystery where you not only have dinner, but you get to follow the characters and be part of a murder mystery. How exciting! You have an opportunity to be entertained and involved for several of hours in an alternate situation that you otherwise would not experience. There are plenty of troupes or restaurants in a wide variety of areas that host Murder Mystery Dinners. Are you the murderer? Go and find out!

C. Act Like A Tourist

Sometimes we are not aware of all the attractions or sites to see in our own area. Then, if family or friends come to town, we check out a few things and take them to the local sites. We live 25 minutes outside of New

York City, yet neither of us have been to the aircraft carrier Intrepid or aboard the Circle Line boats around Manhattan. Yet, Mariann's cousins from Ireland have been. Why don't you and your girlfriend be "tourists for a day." Plan a day visiting the local attractions as if you are brand new to the area. It will be enlightening, and we think you will be surprised at how much you really enjoy experiencing tourist attractions you normally would never see.

Suggestions and information:
- You can visit some travel sites to check out the local attractions:
  > *www.fodors.com/*
  > *www.michelintravel.com/guides-cat/north-america/*
  > *www.travelguidesfree.com/*
- A site for travel and great reviews is Trip Advisor, *www.tripadvisor.com/TravelGuides*

D. Sporting Events

This is a great way to spend a day with your love. Pick a sport you love or one that intrigues you both and take your lady. If you really want to get into the spirit of it, buy yourselves team jerseys or hold up a sign. The theme of the night is sports and good times! Try something new and find a sport that neither of you have ever watched or have been interested in. Get tickets to an event and you may find that you *become* fans of the sport!

E. Make Wine Together

If you and your girlfriend love wine, wineries and wine tasting then you should definitely sign up to make wine together. There are do-it-yourself wineries where you can take lessons and be walked through the wine-making process. Depending on how much of a barrel you buy, you get a certain number of bottles. If you want to invite friends to join in the wine-making festivities and split the finished product, it's even more fun.

Suggestions and information:
- If you have a local winery that offers classes, then sign up. If not, there is a company with regional locations that conducts such classes. Check out California Wine Works *www.cawineworks.com*

Spending time learning about wine and the process is fascinating and informative. When you are done, you get your wine with custom labels. Enjoy coming up with your name and label. When you do, invite a few friends for dinner and celebrate – serving your wine of course!

F. Haunted House

October is Halloween time, and you want to do something amusing with a dash of horror thrown in for the holiday. Sure there are parties, but it's certainly more festive to find a haunted house tour or a haunted mansion where you go in alive and come out scared to death. What is around each corner? Will you make it? Will the ghosts and goblins eat you before you can find the exit? No one knows. Try your luck and see what happens.

There are many areas around this country that are said to be haunted or have been visited by ghosts. Find a haunted house tour or a haunted city tour and be prepared to see a ghost – is that shadowy figure in the street real or a ghost following you? BOO! For example, if you live in Pennsylvania, New Jersey or New York there are many ghost tours. You can travel to nearby New Hope, Pennsylvania which is rich in haunted history. It's fascinating. Other parts of the country share the lore of spirits who are not ready to depart this earth and are waiting to pay a visit to those who stop by their home, business, theater or city. Check your local internet listings in October because many parks, local orchards, farms and other places are transformed into interactive haunted experiences for the holiday.

Suggestions and information:
• If you want to go really scary and visit one of the nation's top real haunted houses, check out a few options from these articles:
 > *homebuilding.thefuntimesguide.com/2011/08/scariest-haunted-houses.php*
 > *www.hauntworld.com/featured_article/americas_best haunted_houses_ scariest_haunted_houses_2012*

G. Christmas Light Tour

Christmas is a busy time of year, and it's easy to get caught up in the swirl of shopping, attending parties and decorating. So, instead of getting overwhelmed by the hustle and bustle and the materialism of the holiday, take a moment to appreciate the magic that illuminates from every decorated house. We all have neighbors or know houses that go above and beyond and some go beyond *above and beyond*. But, take a night to get in the car, put on some Christmas music and just ride around enjoying the various combinations of lights. Some will be stunning or horrifying and others out of this world. This is a nice time to be awestruck by the beauty and magic that is Christmas. Afterwards, find a cozy Irish bar and share a dessert and Bailey's as you warm your hands by the fireplace. It will be a relaxing evening where you can recharge and rediscover the mystique and meaning of Christmas. It is a time of year to be thankful, and is a perfect time to re-connect with each other amid the craziness of the season. Just make sure you both express how grateful you are for each other in your lives.

Suggestions and information:

- Want to see some of the most notable Christmas Lights displays around the country, take a look to see if something is near you:
  > *news.travel.aol.com/2010/11/22/10-best-christmas-light-displays-in-the-us/*
  > *voices.yahoo.com/the-best-holiday-light-displays-united-states-10591065.html?cat=30*

H. 007 Date

Play James Bond to your date's sexy Bond Girl if your budget allows and if you want to pull out all the stops for your theme date. Rent a luxury car, dress in your tuxedo and visit the classiest martini bar in town. You could even combine this type of date with a Scavenger Hunt themed date. Let your date be the "spy" who follows the clues. Finish off with dinner at a five-star restaurant and an overnight stay at a chic hotel.

Suggestions and information:

- Xperience days is a great site because it offers and arranges a variety of exciting 007–like adventures: *www.xperiencedays.com*
- If you live in New York or Miami, you can rent a luxury car and drive in true 007 style: *www.gothamdreamcars.com*

24 Valentine's Day
($ to $$$$ / ♥♥♥ to ♥♥♥♥♥)

Love is in the air on Valentine's Day. Hearts are a flutter with joy and anticipation of sparking a great date and showing your love how you really feel about her.

DATE	COST	ROMANCE
The Surprise Destination	$ - $$$	♥♥♥♥
Peaceful Afternoon Accented By Romantic Dinner	$ - $$$$	♥♥♥
Spa Day	$ - $$$	♥♥♥♥♥
Airborne	$ - $$$	♥♥♥

Things to consider:
- These dates are meant to be romantic for that girl you are happy to call your own.
- These will typically be pricey. But, depending on the activity, you can keep costs down.
- These dates take planning and careful implementation.
- Don't be afraid to be romantic and sweet and go overboard.

Things you may need:

Cell phone, imagination, flowers, candy, jewelry, packing an impromptu overnight bag for you both, reservations.

A. The Surprise Destination

Surprise your honey with a customizable evening out. This date can take two forms. In the first, you ask your lady questions and her answers will (unbeknownst to her) translate to activities to do or places to go on the date. In the second version of the date, you send your lady links to a series of different destinations to pick up pre-planned items (see **Scavenger Hunt** for full details on how to plan this), with the last links sending her to the final destination – *you*!

Why are you asking that?

Send your sweetie a list of questions that are obscure to her but mean something to you. Once she answers, then you can craft a night out around her answers. For example, *"Black or white?"* Black could mean steakhouse and white could mean a seafood restaurant. And, *"Do you prefer hard or soft?"* Where soft could be a restaurant with a view of the water and hard could be view of buildings or a garden, all the while she does not know what it corresponds to. You can make the questions sexy too. For example, *"What length do you like?"* The higher the number the longer the night. You set the ruler. So, if she says 2, that could be just dinner. If she says 7, that could be dinner and a show. If she says 10, maybe dinner and a show and a sexy rendezvous afterwards. Or, *"What is your favorite flavor"* which could correspond to a special dessert presented after dinner. Or, *"What's your favorite position?"* could translate into where you sit in a theater. Or, *"Do you prefer fast and furious or slow and luscious?"* This could correspond to a rock concert vs. a play or symphony. So, when you plan the date tell her that the date was crafted from her answers to your questions. Don't forget the flowers and/or candy. Women love jewelry. Trust us, you can't miss with that!

Where am I going?

The other idea is to send your lady a text with a question. Once she answers correctly, you send her a link of where to go. Perhaps it's a flower shop where there is a bouquet waiting for her. Do two questions with the third question leading her to where you are. You could be at a restaurant or waiting in front of her home with a limo waiting to go anywhere, even the airport. The questions could be anything, but we think it is more romantic if you ask questions about your relationship. For example, *"How long have we been dating?"* or *"On what date did we first kiss?"* or *"Where were we when I first said I Love You?"* She may not like the idea of driving around to meet you somewhere so you could warn her to "amuse me" on this one. She will.

Tips to remember:

• Don't make the destination to destination more than three with the fourth being the final. But, We recommend the third being the last.

- Have fun planning her route and logistics for the evening. Pre-arrange for her to pick up something that is paid for. Don't have her walking around a supermarket and waiting in line.
- Don't have her driving hours to get there.
- The items she gets can be random or deliberate to symbolize your love for her or an experience you both enjoyed. They may be used on your date. That is up to you.

B. Peaceful Afternoon Accented By A Romantic Dinner

Ask yourself what your girl holds dear and brings her peace. Is it an afternoon in the country? Flowers? Whatever she answers, plan a lazy afternoon around that and end with a romantic dinner that fits into the scheme of what she finds peaceful. Perhaps you spend the day driving through the country stopping at antique shops or a general store or working farm. End at a quaint inn and have a leisurely romantic dinner. If you really want to surprise her, book a room and tell her at dinner. Does she love to make things? Perhaps find a rural place that has a pottery class and afterward, head to dinner. Or surprise her by just stopping at an inn then telling her that you made reservations. Are flowers her thing? If yes, plan an afternoon at a botanical garden, and enjoy strolling hand in hand among the rich greenery and vibrant colors. And why not steal a few kisses in between. Afterward, buy her a bouquet of all her favorite flowers. Or, if there is a gift shop, buy her flower themed earrings or other jewelry she may have admired? Make her smile, and surprise her at dinner over candlelight as you gaze into her eyes.

Tips to remember:
- Make this as peaceful and relaxing a day as possible.
- Ramp up your romance with flowers, candy, gift, love note, jewelry or an overnight stay at a quaint inn or hotel.
- Make her feel like she is being taken care of and pampered and that the day is not rushed or overly structured.

C. Spa Day

Men need to embrace the joy of going to the Spa. Many men feel weird walking around in terry cloth robes and having "treatments." But, if you leave that bias aside and open yourself to the Zen aura and relaxation of a spa, then we think you will become a big fan. Women love spas but they also love it when their man is open to going as well. Plan an afternoon of treatments at the spa where you can recline and be pampered as a couple. If you are not sure what treatments to pick, the spa staff will help you for sure with recommendations. If you have the money to spend, then fly your lady to a spa ranch or a resort where you can stay for a couple of days and lounge in luxurious surroundings while being treated like royalty. Depending on your funds, that can be stateside – or not! If you are both not "too relaxed" to go out then perhaps you plan an evening at a cabaret or restaurant with soothing lighting and background music. Pick a place with cloth tablecloths, candles, mood lighting and a warm ambience that provides enough room around your table to dine and have an intimate conversation. If you stay at a hotel perhaps you dine-in.

Tips to remember:

- Some spas have a couple's bath or a packages for you to have treatments together.
- Perfect time to propose. OK, you may not be so sure on where to hide the ring until you give it to her, but we have faith in your resourcefulness. Perhaps while lounging in the hot bath (or natural springs, depending on the spa), you can pop the question.
- Some spas allow and will arrange for champagne to be brought to your relaxation or treatment room. Check with the staff.
- Check out the Spa or know it well. Spa experiences vary. Some salons consider themselves spas, and that is a stretch. Some day spas are OK, but not very luxurious. Pick a spa that offers a relaxation room and is truly a top spa with great amenities and luxury.

Suggestions and information:

- Here is a helpful website for finding a Spa: *www.spafinder.com/*
- Here are some other links that will for finding a Spa or Spa resort:
  > *bestspasusa.com/*
  > *www.huffingtonpost.com/2010/09/25/best-spas-in-america_n_738595.html#s144888&title=1_Inn_at*
  > *www.getawayspas.com/spas_united_states.html*

D. Airborne

Take a helicopter ride over a beautiful area whether it is a big city, Las Vegas or the mountains in Hawaii. Get an aerial view that presents visually stunning sites from another perspective. If you want to propose, do it in flight! Pop some champagne and tell her that your love makes you soar with happiness, and if she would accept your proposal of marriage, you would feel as if you were walking on the clouds. Yes, a bit sappy, but at moments like that, women love it! She'll be telling that story forever. Afterward, arrange a beautiful meal whether it is at a city hotspot, a Vegas 5-star restaurant overlooking the strip, a quaint country inn, or a table for two beachside with torches providing a soft glow (most resorts will arrange this). Make the dinner and ambience right for her or, for you as a couple whether it's down home and comfy, chic and elegant or casual and free.

Suggestions and information:

• You can do an search, ask the hotel concierge at your hotel or use a site such as *www.Xperiencedays.com* to help with ideas or arrangements..

— *Section 3*—

USEFUL
INFORMATION

10 Things You Always Need to Remember

We would like to leave you with ten key things to remember when looking for love and wooing the lady who has caught your eye.

Date.

Give yourself some time to get to know the girl you are dating. If she is sadly not for you, that's OK. That's the purpose of dating. Stay positive and keep at it! Statistics are in your favor that eventually, you will fall in love.

Listen.

Hear what your lady says and remember it — that shows caring and respect. Listening involves remembering and understanding. Women complain that men don't listen. Break that perception and hear what she is saying, which at times involves reading between the lines.

Follow Up.

If you say you are going to call, then do. When you have a date and have just parted, text or call to make sure she got home safely. Don't promise or say something you can't or won't honor. That's not cool. Keep your mouth shut if you can't.

Be Thoughtful.

Thoughtfulness counts and is as important to women as it is to men. Thoughtfulness says you care, are listening, and are sensitive. It shows that you are conscious of your environment and people around you. A little thoughtfulness goes a long, long way.

Be Considerate.

Always be a gentleman. Is your lady cold? Then give her your jacket. Are you going up an unusually steep stair? Take her arm. Crossing a flooded street? Guide her around the huge puddles. Even if she does or says something you don't like, there is a way to communicate respectfully. So, be nice.

Communicate.

Communication is the key to success. A woman can't read a man's mind and a man can't read a woman's mind. It goes both ways. So, if there is something you want, need or have to know, then you need to communicate that. Don't argue or be disrespectful. Whatever the topic, from fun to difficult, it is always better to get it out in the open and discuss it in a mature and open manner.

Be Honest.

Honesty rules! Be honest about how you feel. Don't let things bubble under the surface then erupt in a regrettable way. Be gentle when you communicate especially if the subject is sensitive. If you express your honesty with respect for the other person and in a clear and nice way, it will only help both of you. Whether you want to tell her you love her or want to break up, handle it honestly and with respect and kindness.

Show You Care.

Words only go so far. Actions speak louder than words. If you say you love someone but then disrespect them or are condescending and insulting, then that is not an expression of love. Is she going through a tough time at work? Show you care by listening, helping with suggestions or distracting her with an evening out. Be sensitive to what she is going through whether it is a success or a sad situation and show through your words *and* actions that you care and are there for her.

Originality Is Sexy.

Don't be afraid to be unique, different, quirky or individual. Originality is a great thing. We wish more people were. If you have an idea for a date or outing or vacation, whatever it is, express yourself. It will be appreciated and even if it does not work out as planned, you get an "A" for effort.

It's Always About The Gesture.

We always say it's never about the amount, It's about the gesture. If you buy her a $4000 diamond ring but then are never there for her, talk down to her, take her for granted or are disrespectful, then the ring means nothing.

A meaningful gesture has more worth than an empty grand gift. Once, Mariann was so sick with a stomach virus, she could not get out of bed, and all she wanted was ginger ale. When a friend called to check on her, she said she wanted some ginger ale and was really thirsty. Although he was about to go out to a function in the opposite direction, 30 minutes later she received this text, *"go to your door."* Sitting outside was ginger ale and English muffins, which is all she could consume when ill. She was touched that he had listened and remembered. That little gesture spoke volumes because the friend even modified his plans to help her. That is the kind of gesture that makes her appreciate and love you.

A Little Q & A

Here are a few questions that have been sent in through our articles and blogs. We thought they might cover some of your FAQs.

Should I call her right away after our date?

If you like her – at least text her after the date and let her know you had a good time and want to make sure she got home OK. Even if then takes you a couple of days to reach out again, she won't be feeling abandoned or as though you were not interested. Within three days, reach out and set up your next date.

How often should I see her?

We believe that depends on the intensity of your chemistry and whether you felt an immediate connection. Don't come on so strong that you smother her from day one. If you really like her, and don't want her to get away, then pursue her. If you like her, but are not sure, then continue to see her but pace yourself. I think after a month, you should see each other more than once a week. By three months, you should be spending longer amounts of time together a few times a week. After 3-6 months, We think a guy should know if she's someone you want to continue dating or are serious about. If not, move on. Whichever it is, do not drag out a relationship unnecessarily if you know it is going nowhere. You cause more hurt and make the breakup that much more awkward.

When should I suggest going away together?

That will depend on how much chemistry you have and how quickly the sexual component of your relationship gets started. Ask yourself, *"Do I want to spend a whole weekend with her? Wake up next to her? See her without her makeup? Wait for her to get ready?"* If you answer yes to those questions, then start booking something ASAP. It might be nice to know that she wants to go and then surprise her. If you're at a point in your relationship where you're wondering if it can "go the distance", then a weekend or week together will tell volumes about how you will get on together on a regular, long-term basis.

When should I introduce her to my friends?

When you feel comfortable. Do you like or love her enough to introduce her to your circle of friends? Do you want your friends to like her as much as you do? Or, are you anxious to get a second opinion? Both of us like to date for about a month and get comfortable before we introduce dates to our friends. Our mutual friends are very outgoing, exceptionally witty and sarcastic and can be a little much for the faint of heart. So, we have to make sure the person we are dating can hold his own! Mariann is emphatic for honesty from her friends on their opinions about her new beau. We both respect our good friends who are honest with us whether we like what they say or not. We both take it seriously, filter the input and try to look for issues or warning signs our friends have pointed out. Always listen to your heart and know what is right for you.

How should I introduce her to my parents?

Introducing a girl to your parents is very big – to your girlfriend too. This tells her that you are very serious and that you like her enough to get your parents' approval. If you are on the fence about her, do NOT introduce her yet. She will view an introduction as a big step in the relationship. If you do, then a casual afternoon at your parents' home or yours works well. A nice dinner out where it is not too loud so they can talk and truly get to know each other is a good place to start. We think an environment that is more casual and laid back is much easier. Mariann was introduced to an ex-boyfriend's family at a dinner the night before a wedding shower. It was nice. The next day, she met about 50 cousins, aunts and uncles. So, in one weekend, it was a lot to take in. She would have preferred a gentler introduction over time before meeting his mom and immediate family and all his relatives within a 12 hour period.

How much and to what degree should I romance her?

If you like her then romance her, just don't come on too strong as it can come off as insincere. Don't be needy either. Know what your girl likes and what will make her comfortable and not overwhelmed. Big gestures like a mariachi band at a Mexican restaurant or sending flowers and balloons to her office every day for a month or skywriting "I love you" are all great. But, many times, girls like understated gestures that show you care or listened.

Were you antiquing and noticed she loved a bracelet? Did she find a print that moved her? Does she collect old records and found some she doesn't have? Well, if this is the case, sending that or giving it to her unexpectedly is touching. Sending her a card with a poem you wrote or sweet saying will make her fall harder and quicker. When you show your heart in big and little ways and the thoughtfulness and kindness shine through, your girlfriend will hold on tight and not let you go. It will inspire her to show how much she does love and appreciates you. To make her feel special, desired and pretty is sexy and romantic to her. But remember it is the little gestures that make big impressions like offering her your jacket if you notice she is cold. Offering to change seats with her if you notice the sunlight is in her eyes. Sending her a text to make sure she got home OK from an event. Bringing over some chicken soup, crackers and ginger ale (even if you leave it at the door) when she has told you she went home from work sick. Thoughtfulness is very romantic to women. When in doubt, go subtle and thoughtful.

What are the "deal breakers"?

You need to know your deal breakers going into any relationship. Keep your eyes wide open for the signs. If red flags are coming up like fireworks, then perhaps you need to end the relationship. Don't make excuses for her if you see a lot of deal breakers manifesting. Either accept it and move forward or move on. Mariann has a few deal breakers which shut down her feelings such as cheapness, laziness, lack of thoughtfulness, rudeness and crudeness. It differs for everyone. But, think about yours. Know what they are. Then stand by them and find someone who encompasses all you want and deserve in a soul mate.

Ways To Say I Love You

There are many ways to express your love, your feelings or how much you care. We know that many men have trouble saying the words, "I Love You". Here are some ideas or suggestions that convey "I Love You". And, by all means, add your own ideas to this list.

- Flowers (local store or FTD)
- Fruit arrangement (Edible Arrangements has some great options)
- Love IOUs
- Write a poem
- Sexy notes
- Mail romantic cards
- Jewelry
- Memento – a meaningful gift that marks a special moment or feeling
- Pandora bracelet – get a bead that has a special meaning for her
- Skywriting, "I Love You"
- Meaningful gestures
- Being there with help when she needs it
- Being sensitive to a difficult time and supporting her or creating a distraction (could be as simple as having a home cooked meal ready or picking up her laundry or having her house cleaned).
- Spend a day pampering her or doing her errands
- Sexy text
- Coupons of Love — she can cash them in anytime she wants. They can range from washing her car to a foot massage to anything you want a coupon to say.
- Make a CD of her favorite music
- Make a home movie with her in it
- Create a photo album of your adventure or of your relationship
- Create a "Memory Book" which is a combo of photos and symbols (pressed flowers, stickers) – a bit like scrapbooking. Michael's, for example is a craft store and a good place for the book and supplies.
- Have a puzzle made that says I LOVE YOU or WILL YOU MARRY ME?– assemble it together during a quiet evening at home. Get a custom crossword puzzle made. (See the appendix of websites for some useful custom puzzle websites).

Dating In The Digital Age

We live in a great time with all the electronic devices that allow easy communication and access to information within seconds. But, we will give you one word of caution — you are not dating your cell phone. I know in this technological age, we are all connected to our cell phones, iPads and electronic gadgets. Just remember, there is a time and place for everything. The cell phone can be your friend - you can send texts to make sure your date got home or sexy texts once you are in a relationship. But, when you are on a date with someone ... *be on the date*. Don't constantly be checking your phone, updating your Facebook status or leaving it out on the table. Its' just rude and it's not respectful. Also, don't use texting and email as a replacement for speaking on the phone and meeting in person. *Facetime* on your iPhone is great, but it's much better in person. Mariann did this with a recent relationship where most of their communication was electronic. Whereas it connected them on one level, it encouraged a relationship that lacked the depth and true connection talking and in-person meetings bring. Be present in the moment with the person you are dating.

When your cell phone rings, don't feel obligated to answer. Sure, you can glance at it to see if it's a call that you must take. If it is, then do. If it's your parent or child, then by all means take the call. But, if it's your friend who calls you three times a day to discuss who won the football game — don't pick it up and focus on your date!

I don't know a person who is not on Facebook. Yes, it is very important to check Facebook to find out that someone has gone to the doctor's, or see a cute picture of some puppy you don't know or learn that your friends are glad it's Friday! In the scheme of life - these are all unimportant distractions. Sure, if you have some time to kill waiting for takeout or are at home at night and want to peruse some posts to see what people are doing — great. When you are with someone you care about, your priority is to focus on them and the development of your relationship.

Mariann is an open person but does not believe in posting every thought or thing she does on Facebook. She treasures her privacy and not everything is worthy of posting. She once dated someone who never used his phone on a date — she loved this! His focus was on her. Once he got a smart phone though, he was constantly on Facebook and checking his email and texts. It was annoying because he would do that in the middle of a conversation. What kind of message does that send? Mariann felt what she was saying was uninteresting or unimportant. She was very open with him that she rarely posts about where she is or who she is with. Yet her boyfriend got mad and pouty when she didn't post that she was out on a date with him. He was missing the point — she was with him there and now. Actions speak louder than words. She felt her action of *being with him* spoke louder than some lame Facebook post.

Use your phone and electronics appropriately. Make them work for you to stay in touch, take a picture and access information, but not to replace real life interaction. When you are with your date — be with your date. If your date is constantly using their phone excessively, then be honest that you prefer you both focus on each other and agree to limit use when you are together. We gotta go ... our cell phone is ringing!

Websites for Date Planning

Aquarium

www.touristinformationdirectory.com/united_states/Aquariums/public_aquarium.htm

Amusement Parks

www.sixflags.com/national/index.aspx

themeparks.about.com/cs/usparks/l/blparksbystate.htm

Antiquing

www.antiquetrail.com/

www.usa-antiquestores.com/

www.antiquetheusa.com/

www.usantiquedealer.com

antiquesacrosstheus.com/

Arcades

www.daveandbusters.com/default.aspx

www.arcadepages.info/

Astrology

www.astrologyzone.com

www.karmicrelief.com

Bakeries - Custom / Specialty / Themed

www.carlosbakery.com

Bakeries - Erotic

www.theeroticbakery.com

www.eroticbakery.net/erotic_cakes_usa_locations.html

Bars and Restaurants

www.bubblelounge.com

www.worldsbestbars.com

www.foodandwine.com/slideshows/americas-best-bars
www.travel.yahoo.com/ideas/America-s-best-wine-bars.html
www.oneifbyland.com
www.ayzanyc.com

Bed & Breakfasts

www.bedandbreakfast.com/usa.html
www.resortsandlodges.com/bed-and-breakfasts/usa/index.html
www.bbon-line.com/united-states/

Beer

www.craftbeer.com
www.beefinfo.com
www.brewersassociation.org
voices.yahoo.com/top-10-beer-festivals-united-states-4068635.html
www.cnbc.com/id/39233398/The_10_Biggest_US_Craft_Breweries
www.beercrafting.com

Caverns

cavern.com/
www.touristinformationdirectory.com/cave/list_of_caves.htm
www.showcaves.com/english/usa/region/ByRegion.html

Civil War Re-Enactment

reenactmenthq.com/
www.civilwartraveler.com/events/

Cooking

www.iceculinary.com

Christmas Lights

news.travel.aol.com/2010/11/22/10-best-christmas-light-displays-in-the-us/
voices.yahoo.com/the-best-holiday-light-displays-united-states-10591065.
html?cat=30

Country Fair

www.renfaire.com

Dining and Dining Services (Date Staging)

www.by-michelle.com
www.camaje.com/specialevents.html
la.darkdining.com/
newyork.danslenoir.com/
www.goldstar.com

Dinner Cruises

www.worldyacht.com/site/home.aspx
www.hornblower.com/hce/home
www.victorycasinocruises.com
www.ehow.com/list_5976902_louisiana-riverboat-casinos.html

Entertainment

www.zagat.com
www.yelp.com
www.goldstar.com
www.groupon.com
www.bloomspot.com

Experiences

www.xperiencedays.com

Flowers

www.ftd.com

Food and Chocolate Shows

www.tradefairdates.com/Trade-Shows-for-Sweets-Chocolate-Y326-S1.html

Gambling

www.ehow.com/list_5976902_louisiana-riverboat-casinos.html
www.worldcasinodirectory.com/new-jersey/casino-list
www.uscasinocity.com

Gift Baskets

www.ediblearrangements
www.gourmetgiftbaskets.com

Gun Range

machinegunsvegas.com/about-us/ .

Yoga

www.kripalu.org
www.retreatfinder.com

Games – Adult Board Games

www.lingeriediva.com/lingerie-accessories/adult-board-games
www.boardgamecentral.com/games/adult.html

Hangover Remedy

www.mercydrink.com

Historical Villages

www.antiquing.com/historic.htm
www.cr.nps.gov/nr/
www.colonialwilliamsburg.com
allairevillage.org/
batstovillage.org/
www.historicsmithvillenj.com/

Horseback Riding

www.horserentals.com/horses.html
www.horseshowcentral.com/horse_stables.php
www.horseandtravel.com/

Helicopter Rides

www.xperiencedays.com

Haunted Houses

homebuilding.thefuntimesguide.com/2011/08/scariest-haunted-houses.php
www.hauntworld.com/featured_article/americas_best_haunted_houses_scariest_haunted_houses_2012

Ice Hotels

www.icehotel.com
www.hoteldeglace-canada.com/

Interior Design/Event Planning

www.by-michelle.com

Love Coupons

www.rom101.com/lovecoupons.jsp
couponsformylover.com/love-coupons.aspx
www.withluv.com/printables/love-coupons.aspx

Music Festivals

http://www.thespacelab.tv/spaceLAB/theSHOW/Spacelab-MusicFestivals.htm
musicusafestivals.org
www.festivals.com
www.festivalfinder.com
www.festivals-and-shows.com/music-festivals.html

Memory Book

www.michaels.com

Museum of Sex

www.museumofsex.com/
www.eroticheritagemuseumlasvegas.com/
en.wikipedia.org/wiki/Sex_museum#cite_note-3

Museums

www.usa.gov/Citizen/Topics/History-Museums.shtml
www.museumsusa.org/museums/
www.museumsusa.org/museums/

www.artcyclopedia.com/museums-us.html

museumca.org

www.museumsusa.org/museums/

www.aero.com/museums/museums.htm

airandspace.si.edu/

sandiegoairandspace.org/

www.vasc.org

www.aero.com/museums/museums.htm

www.nationalmuseum.af.mil

www.tulsaairandspacemuseum.org/index.php

airandspacemuseum.org

www.evergreenmuseum.org/

www.armstrongmuseum.org

intrepidmuseum.org

www.spymuseum.org/

www.madametussauds.com/washington/

dir.yahoo.com/arts/humanities/history/museums_and_memorials/wax_museums /?skw=listings+of+wax+museums+in+the+USA

www.ripleys.com

www.artsmart.com(customized museum tours)

Olympics

www.olympic.org/united-states-of-america

en.wikipedia.org/wiki/List_of_Olympic_Games_host_cities

Off Road / All Terrain Vehicles

www.treadlightly.org

ezinearticles.com/?Off-Road-Vehicle-Safety---Ten-Tips-to-Increase-Safety&id=2557059

www.atvsafety.org/InfoSheets/ATV_Riding_Tips.pdf

www.artipot.com/articles/1443840/tips-for-safety-while-riding-an-off-road-vehicle.htm

On-line Dating Sites

www.singleswarehouse.co.uk

www.match.com

www.eharmony.com

www.catholicmatch.com

www.ourtime.com

www.jdate.com

www.zoosk.com

www.pof.com

www.okcupid.com

Planetariums

en.wikipedia.org/wiki/List_of_planetariums

www.touristinformationdirectory.com/Planetarium/Science_Center_Observatory_planetariums_US.htm

Puzzles

www.piczzle.com

www.zazzle.com

www.custompuzzles.com (custom crossword puzzle)

Racetrack

www.officialusa.com/stateguides/horseracingtracks/index.html

Race Cars / Luxury Cars

www.xperiencedays.com

www.gothamdreamcars.com

Scavenger Hunt

www.accomplicetheshow.com

www.wikihow.com/Propose-to-Her-Using-a-Scavenger-Hunt-Gam

www.mymysteryparty.com/scavengerhunts.html

www.wikihow.com/Play-a-Scavenger-Hunt-Game-at-a-Party

www.buzzle.com/articles/scavenger-hunt-ideas-for-adults.html

games.thefuntimesguide.com/2011/09/scavenger-hunts.php

www.ehow.com/how_7764118_set-up-scavenger-hunt-wife.html

www.scavenger-hunt-guru.com/romantic-scavenger-hunt.html

Shakespeare

bbbard.com/index.php
www.shakespearefellowship.org/linksfestivals.htm
en.wikipedia.org/wiki/Bard_on_the_Beach
www.bardonthebeach.org
shakespeare.palomar.edu/festivals.htm
www.outdoordrama.org/about/

Spas/Massages

www.spabodyworkmarket.com
www.luxurysparobes.com
www.target.com/c/accessories-spa-massage-health-beauty/-/N-5xtz8
www.spafinder.com/
bestspasusa.com/
www.huffingtonpost.com/2010/09/25/best-spas-in-america_n_738595.
html#s144888&title=1_Inn_at
www.getawayspas.com/spas_united_states.html

Search Engines

www.google.com
www.yahoo.com
www.ask.com
www.bing.com

Sex Shops / Adult / Lingerie

www.mypleasure.com
www.romantixon-line.com
www.thepleasurechest.com
www.myla.com
www.kikidm.com
www.fredericks.com
www.hustlerstore.com
www.lingeriediva.com/lingerie-accessories/adult-board-games
www.boardgamecentral.com/games/adult.html

Social Groups

www.meetup.com
www.newyorksocialnetwork.com

Space Camp / Aviation

www.spacecamp.com/
www.spacecamp.com/adults
www.nasa.gov/centers/kennedy/about/information/camp_faq.html
www.kennedyspacecenter.com/program-inquiry.aspx

Tickets

www.ticketmaster.com
www.telecharge.com
www.theatermania.com
www.playbill.com

Travel / Tourist

www.travelzoo.com
www.expedia.com
www.jetsetter.com
www.orbitz.com
www.groupon.com
www.bloomspot.com
www.fodors.com
www.michelintravel.com/guides-cat/north-america/
www.tripadvisor.com/TravelGuides
www.tripadvisor.com

Table Setting

www.ehow.com/how_2338210_set-table-romantic-dinner.html

Vegas

www.vegas.com/attractions/
govegas.about.com/od/attractions/a/100thingstodo.htm
www.tripadvisor.com/Attractions-g45963-Activities-Las_Vegas_Nevada.html

Video Services

www.rgibs.com
www.motophoto.com

Water Parks

themeparks.about.com/cs/waterparks/l/blwaterparksst.htm
www.ultimatewaterpark.com/waterparks/parks_by_state.php
www.waterparks.com/default.asp

Wine / Wine Tasting

www.cawineworks.com
americaswinetrails.com/
www.winetrailsusa.com/

Zoos

www.officialusa.com/stateguides/zoos/
www.unitedstatestouristattractions.com/content/top_zoos_in_the_united_states.html

What To Do Between Relationships

If your goal is to find your soul mate, then you need to know your comfort zone, then seek out activities or venues to find that person. Some people are most comfortable behind a computer and that is fine. We suggest you participate in multiple venues or paths to meeting people. One of those paths should be live interaction with others. People tend to get too isolated behind the solitary confinement and anonymity of the computer screen. For example, join a political or charity organization focused on an issue you care about (e.g.. Cancer Cares, Alzheimer's, Habitat for Humanity, Child Trafficking), join an athletic club (e.g. hiking, triathlon training, tennis), a religious social group or social network to meet friends/dates (e.g. NY Social Network, Meetup) or even go to singles events (e.g. wine tasting, Match Stir events, rotating seat dinner, bowling), speed dating or singles dances. Wherever your interests lie such as politics, fundraising, religion, sports, sailing, cooking, cuisine or dining out, there are groups you can join to meet like-minded people.

Like to hike or rock climb or jump out of airplanes? Well, there are adventure oriented singles organizations that bring the thrill of such activities to their members. If you live in or near a city, and just want to make friends or possibly find a date, there are several social networking groups available. New York Social Network in NYC (*www.newyorksocialnetwork.com*) plans activities every day from tennis to bowling to wine tasting to concerts and movie nights so people can have a secure and fun environment to get to know other people. Love wine? There are single wine tasting groups. *www.meetup.com* is a nationwide website that has regional groups in many categories. Groups are led by volunteer event organizers. You can go on-line and see what interests you in your area, or you can become an event organizer yourself if you have the ambition and capability. Are you a foodie? Most cities have cooking schools or many restaurants offer cooking classes. Often, they revolve around "single cooking classes." We've both tried speed dating and shockingly, you can tell in 7 or 8 minutes if you like someone and want to see them again. Funny as it sounds, it is true. The important thing to remember is to be active., Interact with people, and do things that interest you so that whether you meet someone or not, at least you are enjoying yourself.

If you are wondering how to meet people, here are some suggestions:

- On-line dating sites (Singles Warehouse, Match, eHarmony, Plenty of Fish, OKCupid, JDate, Catholic Singles, Zoosk)
- Speed dating
- Social network / Friend networking groups
- Cooking classes
- Meet up groups according to your likes (www.meetup.com)
- Religious singles socials
- Political party groups / Campaigns / Action groups
- Charities
- Ask your friends to set you up — Let them know you are looking
- Business networking groups or sponsored through your regional chamber of commerce
- Industry organizations and industry networking events
- Sailing – take lessons – join a sailing club
- Sports (hiking, tennis, rock climbing, softball teams, bowling leagues)
- Singles dances, events, cruises or vacations

So, check out your local papers, regional magazines or the internet to investigate the above and how to get involved.

Some Sexy Recipes

If Mamma didn't pass on her kitchen skills, here are some recipe selections that can be a good place to start. An internet search or visit to the Cookbook section of the local bookstore will also help. There are a few things you should consider when cooking a sexy meal for your date or loved one:

- Either plan a simple full meal or a meal of small easy bites
- Don't let the cooking keep you from time with your date or from conversation
- Be careful of what you cook and how it affects your breath or stomach. Onion soup is yummy but not a friend to your breath and it can be gassy – so be careful as bad breath is a romance killer
- Be careful with food that's too spicy — may not sit well with your date
- Red wine is great, but it can stain lips and teeth so pay attention to that
- Try to cook with foods that are considered an aphrodisiacs such as garlic, strawberries, chocolate, champagne, ginger, saffron, oysters, figs, basil, celery, bananas, hot chilies, avocados, pomegranates, red wine, salmon, walnuts, vanilla, watermelon, honey, fennel, nutmeg, mustard, truffles, raspberries, licorice, and asparagus.
- Stay away from soy and cilantro since they are libido killers
- Try to create a very romantic ambience with nice tablecloth, candles, flowers, plates, soothing music and appealing fragrances
- Try to keep the food courses light. You don't want anything so heavy it will sit in one's stomach or get one sluggish or tired
- Try to pick foods that don't have bones

Appetizers

Apple-Goat Cheese Bruschetta
Total 20 minutes prep time

Ingredients
4 slices French bread (1/2 inch thick)
1 small Fuji apple, chopped
1/8 cup crumbled goat cheese
1/2 teaspoon minced fresh thyme
1/4 teaspoon minced fresh oregano
1/8 teaspoon coarsely ground pepper

Directions
Place bread slices on an ungreased baking sheet. Broil 3-4 in. from the heat for 1-2 minutes or until golden brown. Combine the apple, goat cheese, thyme, oregano and pepper; sprinkle over bread. Broil 1 minute longer or until cheese is softened. Yield: 8 appetizers.

Melon, Mozzarella and Prosciutto Skewers
Total 10 minutes prep time

Ingredients
Cantaloupe, cubed or balled
Fresh Basil Leaves
Bocacinni (mozzarella balls)
Prosciutto (Italian ham)
Extra Virgin Olive Oil
A pinch of salt
Wooden Skewers

Directions
Put a layer of melon, basil, bocacinni, and prosciuttol onto a skewer. Drizzle with olive oil and salt. Garnish with diced basil. Serve cold.

Bacon Breadsticks

Total time 30 minutes

Ingredients

3 bacon strips, halved lengthwise

6 breadsticks (about 5 inches long)

Directions

Wrap a piece of bacon around each breadstick. Place on a rack in an ungreased 15-in. x 10-in. x 1-in. baking pan. Bake at 375° for 20-25 minutes or until bacon is crisp. Yield: 6 pcs.

Baked Cheddar Olives

Total 15 minutes prep time, 15 minutes to cook

Ingredients

2 cups grated sharp cheddar

1 cup flour

1/4 teaspoon cayenne

8 tablespoons softened butter

40 small green olives with pimento, drained and patted dry

Directions

Stir 1st three ingredients together. Work in softened butter to form dough. Drop dollop of dough on wax paper and place an olive in middle. Flour hands and roll olive in between your palms to cover olive. Place all olives on a cookie sheet.

Bake 15 minutes. Serve warm.

Bacon and Lettuce Stuffed Cherry Tomatoes

Total 20 minutes prep time

Ingredients

20 Cherry tomatoes
¼ cup chopped fresh chives or ¼ cup chopped green onions
10 slices of bacon fried crisp and broken up (try precooked bacon)
½ cup lettuce very finely chopped
3 Tablespoons of mayonnaise
Salt & Pepper

Directions

Cut the top off the tomatoes and scoop out the seeds and the pulp.

Salt the inside of the tomatoes and put them upside down on a paper to drain for about for 15 minutes. Meanwhile, combine the lettuce, chives, bacon and mayo. Season with salt and pepper. But remember, you have already salted the tomatoes. Fill the tomatoes just before serving.

Mixed Greens with Raspberries, Almonds and Vinaigrette

Total 15 minutes prep time

Ingredients

Chopped romaine lettuce
Herb goat cheese
Raspberries
Slivered almonds
A dash of olive oil and some balsamic vinegar
For something a bit heavier you could add grilled chicken or salmon

Directions

Combine all ingredients in a bowl. Serve and enjoy!

The World's Smoothest Guacamole (made with sour cream)

Total 5 minutes prep time

Ingredients

2 avocados, pulp of

2 limes, juice of

1 garlic clove

1 small tomato, diced

½ cup red onion, diced

½ teaspoon of roasted ground cumin

Sea salt

Cayenne pepper

2 tablespoons of sour cream

Directions

Mash the avocado pulp with a potato masher or fork . Using the fork, whisk in the remaining ingredients except for the sour cream (or you can do it in the food processor for an even silkier texture.)

Let stand at room temperature for 15 minutes. Whisk in the sour cream, and you are ready to serve. Serve with corn chips

Naughty Nachos

Total 15 minutes prep time

Ingredients

1 pound of ground beef
1 white onion, chopped
1 packet of taco seasoning
tortilla chips, a whole bunch
1 seeded tomato diced
1/4 cup red onion, diced
3 green onions, diced
black olives, sliced
sour cream
guacamole
1 jalapeno pepper, sliced and seeded
cheddar cheese
jack cheese

Directions

In a large skillet over medium-high heat, brown the ground beef with the white onion. Pour off fat and stir in taco seasoning. Spoon meat onto a large plate of tortilla chips. Add tomato, red onion, green onion, cheese, jalapenos, and black olives. Microwave until melted.

Top with guacamole and sour cream.

Dinners

Quick and Easy Chicken Marsala

Total 25 minutes prep time

Ingredients

4 chicken breast halves, boneless, skinless
1/4 cup all-purpose flour (for coating)
1/2 teaspoon salt
1/4 teaspoon ground black pepper
1/2 teaspoon dried oregano
1/4 cup olive oil
1/4 cup butter
1 cup fresh mushrooms, sliced
1/2 cup Marsala wine
1/4 cup cream sherry

Directions

Pound chicken breasts until flat and thin. Set aside.

Mix together the flour, salt, pepper, and oregano in a pie pan. Melt oil and butter in a large skillet and bring to a low boil.

Dredge chicken until thoroughly coated by the flour mixture, shake off excess and lightly brown in skillet about 2 minutes. Turn over chicken pieces and add mushrooms

Cook until lightly browned. Add wine and sherry. Cover skillet and simmer for 10 minutes, turning chicken pieces once

Serve with steamed vegetables or a crisp green salad.

As long as you bought the Marsala, serve it to her in a little glass as a sweet after-dinner drink

Broiled Lobster Tails with Garlic-Chili Butter

Total 15 minutes prep time / 30 minutes cook time

Ingredients

4 8-ounce fresh or frozen lobster tails
1 teaspoon finely shredded orange peel
½ teaspoon chili powder
1 clove garlic, minced
¼ cup butter
(clarified butter option)

Directions

Thaw lobster tails, if frozen. Preheat butter. Butterfly the lobster tails by cutting through the center of the hard top shells and meat. Spread the halves of the tails apart. Place lobster tails, meat side up, on the unheated rack of a broiler pan.

In a small skillet cook garlic, orange peel and chili powder in butter over medium heat about 30 seconds or until garlic is tender. Don't let it get brown. Brush mixture over lobster meat.

Broil 4 inches from heat for 12 to 14 minutes or until lobster meat is opaque. If desired, serve with clarified butter.

Makes 4 lobster tails.

A note about Clarified Butter:

Whole butter is clarified by melting it to separate it into three layers. The bottom layer is the undesirable milk solids, the middle is clarified butter and water is at the top. As it cooks, the water will turn to steam and escape, leaving behind the pure butterfat floating on top of the milk solids. Once the butter has completely separated in the pan, carefully pour the mixture through several layers of cheesecloth to strain out the solids, retaining only the butterfat. This is clarified butter. From an entire pound of butter, you will only get 1 1/2 cups of clarified butter, because the milk solids account for the remaining volume.

You'll impress her with your skill and knowledge.

Grilled Steak with Avocado Tomato Salad

Total 10 minutes prep time / 20 minutes cook time

Ingredients

2 avocados
1 cup grape tomatoes
1-1/2 cups mixed salad greens
1/4 cup ranch or honey Dijon salad dressing
4 rib eye or tenderloin steaks
Salt and pepper to taste

Directions

Prepare and preheat grill, or broiler.

Meanwhile, peel avocados and chop. Combine with tomatoes and greens in serving bowl. Drizzle with salad dressing and toss

Season steaks with salt and pepper and grill or broil until desired doneness Place on serving plate and top each steak with some of the avocado mixture. Serve immediately. Serves 4

Mini Tapenade and Manchego Sandwiches

(These are sandwiches made with toasted baguettes, meltable sheep's-milk cheese, briny tapenade, and peppery arugula)

Total 20 minutes prep time

Ingredients

1/3 cup Mixed Olive Tapenade
1 sweet baguette, sliced in half horizontally (That's the small diameter French bread)
4 ounces aged Manchego cheese, shredded (about 1 1/2 cups).
1 ounce arugula leaves (about 1 1/2 packed cups)

Note You can prepare up to 3 days in advance to make things easier. Mix up (or buy) the tapenade, shred the cheese, and wash the arugula leaves (then store them in the refrigerator wrapped in damp paper towels placed in a re-sealable plastic bag) Assemble and broil the sandwich at the last minute. Can't find Manchego? Pecorino, Romano and Asiago are options

Directions

Heat the broiler to high and arrange a rack in the middle.

Evenly spread tapenade on cut sides of baguette halves. Evenly sprinkle cheese over tapenade. Place baguette halves on a baking sheet cut sides up, and broil until the cheese is melted and bubbly and the edges of the bread are toasted, about 2 minutes. Top with arugula, close sandwich, and cut into appropriately sized pieces.

Simple Shrimp Scampi for Two

Total 25 minutes prep time

Ingredients

4 ounces uncooked linguine
2 small garlic cloves, minced
2 tablespoons butter
2 tablespoons olive oil
2 tablespoons lemon juice
1/4 teaspoon Italian seasoning
12 large shrimp, peeled and deveined

Directions

Cook linguine according to package directions. Meanwhile, in a small nonstick skillet, cook garlic in butter and oil until golden. Stir in the lemon juice, Italian seasoning and shrimp; heat till shrimp is just done – about 5 minutes.
Drain linguine; toss with shrimp mixture.
A salad with Italian vinaigrette and bread sticks complete the meal.

Dessert

Strawberries Romanoff

Total 15 minutes prep time

Ingredients

1-2 pounds fresh strawberries (do not use frozen strawberries)
Confectioner's Sugar
Grand Marnier
Vanilla Ice Cream

Directions

Clean the strawberries and take off green stems. If the strawberries are very large, cut in half. Put strawberries in a mixing bowl. Pour a few ounces of Grand Marnier over strawberries

Gently toss the strawberries in the Grand Marnier so they all come in contact with the liquid. Pour a few tablespoons of confectioner's sugar over the strawberries. With a spatula, gently toss or move the strawberries around in the sugar/liqueur mix.

The sugar should be mixed with the liquid till it is a smooth and syrupy sauce without being too thick. There should be no lumps.

If you feel you want more sauce, just add more Grand Marnier and sugar. Taste in between to ensure it is not too sweet or too liqueur tasting. It should be a nice blend. No ingredient should overwhelm the other.

Mix the strawberries in the mixture so all of them have been touched by the sauce. Put some plastic wrap over top. Put in refrigerator and let them marinate for 2-4 hours.

When time for dessert put a couple of scoops of vanilla ice cream in a bowl. Top the ice cream with 3-6 strawberries .

Pour a tablespoon or two of the syrup/sauce over strawberries and ice cream. Serve. You can put a dollop of whip cream on top, but if you do, not too much.

You can substitute any orange based liqueur for Grand Marnier.

Couldn't Be Simpler Sherbert

Total 10 minutes prep time

Ingredients

Store bought sherbet (or Italian ice)
Fresh berries (Raspberries, Blueberries, Blackberries or Sliced Strawberries)
Fresh Mint.

Directions

Place a large scoop of sherbet in a cut glass bowl. Top with fresh berries and a sprig of mint.

Incredibly Simple Fudge

10 minutes prep time / 2 hours chill time

Ingredients

1 (14 ounce) can sweetened condensed milk
12 ounces dark chocolate
1 dash vanilla extract

Directions

Break the chocolate into pieces and melt together with the milk. This can either be done in the top of a double boiler or in the microwave. Stir until smooth. Add the vanilla and stir again

Spray an 8 x 8 inch pan with vegetable oil spray

Pour in the fudge and smooth over the top. Don't forget to lick the bowl!

Chill in the refrigerator for about two hours. Cut into squares.

She'll be so impressed that you made this from scratch especially for her. Send her home with the remainder tied in a fancy napkin

Tasty Cocktails

Lorraine's Luscious and Lovely Limoncello

(need to prepare a week before serving)

20 minutes prep time / 1 week to let stand/infuse / 15 minutes cook time

Ingredients

750 ml of vodka (26 fluid ounces)
6 lemons
1 ¾ cups of sugar
750 ml of water

Directions

Wash the lemons, using soap, rinse well. Peel the lemons. You can use a Microplane Zester or a potato peeler. Make sure not to get any of the bitter white pith. Place the peel in a bowl and cover with the vodka. A large Tupperware bowl with a cover works great

Let the lemons infuse in the vodka for one week

Line a strainer with paper towels and strain the lemony vodka into a bowl that will hold more than twice its volume. Mix the sugar with the water in a heavy-bottomed pot and let it come to a boil. Boil for 2 minutes, giving it an occasional stir

Let cool

Add the sugar syrup to the lemon vodka and mix. Place in your favorite bottle. Keep the Limoncello in the freezer (it won't freeze).

Serve and enjoy!

Liquid Skittles

10 minutes prep time

Ingredients

6 ounces Malibu mango rum (1/4 cup plus 2 tablespoons)
12 ounces strawberries, daiquiri frozen mix or 12 ounces cherry limeade
6 ounces lemon lime Gatorade (1/4 cup plus 2 tablespoons)

Directions

Mix all ingredients together. Serve and enjoy!

Mississippi Mudslide

10 minutes prep time

Ingredients

1 pint chocolate ice cream
1 pint coffee ice cream
1 cup milk
½ cup Bourbon
Her favorite topping or
Whipped cream
Chocolate syrup
Toasted marshmallow

Directions

Put the ice cream, milk and bourbon in a blender. Blend until smooth.

Serve with toppings and enjoy